This book is to be returned on or before
the last date stamped below.

2/2

1 M

1 3 OCT 1986

University of Strathclyde

The Andersonian Library

ML

backyard
fish farming

ANDERSONIAN LIBRARY
★
WITHDRAWN
FROM
LIBRARY
STOCK
★
UNIVERSITY OF STRATHCLYDE

paul bryant
kim jauncey
and tim atack

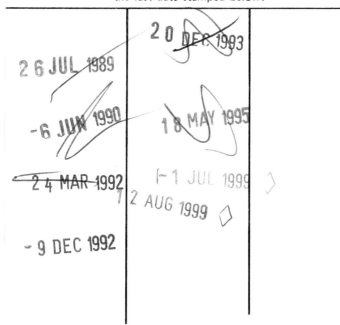
prism press

Published in 1980 by
PRISM PRESS
Stable Court
Chalmington
Dorchester
Dorset DT2 0HB

Copyright Paul Bryant, Kim Jauncey, Tim Atack, 1980
Illustrations by Stephen Cox

ISBN 0 904727 23 8 Hardback
ISBN 0 904727 24 6 Paperback

Printed in Great Britain by
UNWIN BROTHERS LIMITED
The Gresham Press, Old Woking, Surrey

contents

acknowledgements

We would like to thank all our friends and colleagues at the University of Aston in Birmingham whose valuable criticisms of our efforts were greatly appreciated. Particular thanks are also due to Colin Spooner of Prism Press, who made the production of this book possible, and our respective wives for their patience, help and forbearance throughout.

Paul Bryant
Tim Atack
Kim Jauncey

introduction

Fish have been farmed in Europe and Asia for centuries and although for various social and economic reasons methods have changed, our first reason for farming remains: we like eating fish.

Choice of species is however determined mainly by economic considerations concentrating on those with a high commercial value. Fish farming is attractive for more than purely economic reasons since fish represent a harvestable part of the aquatic ecosystem which is otherwise difficult to exploit.

We have gradually developed a sedentary agricultural life-style; yet we still revert to the more primitive hunter-gatherer approach when catching fish. Through consistent over-fishing of natural freshwater and marine stocks, we have depleted them almost to the point where they are no longer self-sustaining, and face a drastic reduction in this traditional food source. The substitution of a more civilised husbandry for existing practices is therefore imperative, if only to avoid future cod wars.

The aims of modern fish farming are similar to those of agriculture, but with some very important differences. 1. Impounding water with the intention of keeping fish really constitutes the creation of a new environment — conventional agriculture makes use of the existing environment. 2. Fish culture involves another dimension, that of volume. It can thus be more productive than conventional livestock rearing on the same area of land — rather like rearing sheep in a multi-storey building! 3. Aquaculture can make use of marginal land, such as marsh, otherwise unsuitable for agricultural development. 4. It is also a more efficient food production system than most other types of animal farming.

Proportionally, fish contain a greater amount of edible flesh than pigs, sheep, cattle, etc., and need to eat a smaller quantity of food to

1

produce this flesh. In other words, to produce one pound of meat, a cow would need to consume about 20 pounds of food, a chicken around 5 pounds, while a fish would need as little as two. This high efficiency of food conversion is partly due to fish being cold-blooded (poikilothermic). Assuming the temperature of their surroundings, they do not have to burn energy to keep warm, and this saving may be expressed as growth. The buoyancy of their watery environment also reduces the energy requirement for movement and support — they never have hills to climb!

However, their excellent food conversion efficiency is also partly due to the quality of their diet and this leads us to the first *disadvantage* of farming fish. 1. The proportion of protein in the diet of ruminants is low, and they live mainly off food sources unusable directly by man, especially in poorer countries. In contrast, most fish need a fairly high percentage of protein in their diet. 2. The constant nature of an aquatic environment has meant that fish have not had to develop the robustness that characterises land animals, and they are thus prone to a wide range of diseases, parasites and predators. They can also tolerate only relatively small changes in their physical environment. The evolutionary answer to these problems has been an incredibly high reproduction rate, but this is of little practical use to the fish farmer when outbreak of a disease can mean destruction of the entire stock. 3. On any intensive basis, the capital cost of setting up a fish farm is considerable: as is the degree of attention required in day-to-day running of the farm.

The disadvantages of aquaculture by no means outweigh the potential benefits, and for the forseeable future it will have an increasingly important place amongst animal husbandry industries.

The Small-scale Fish Farm

Fish culture is traditionally carried out in ponds, which can vary greatly in size, shape, complexity, and system of management. At one extreme, fish ponds can be stocked very densely with fish fed exclusively on an artificial diet (intensive farming), while at the other, they can be occasionally stocked with a few wild fish and equally occasionally culled (extensive farming).

Since we are discussing fish farming on a small scale, only the more efficient methods are applicable, and we have ignored extensive methods of culture. The basic requirements for a fish farm are an adequate supply of pure water and a suitable site for construction. With ingenuity of design, these constraints are not as limiting as they might appear. It is quite possible to keep and rear fish for home consumption in a very small area indeed, in the order of a few square yards. Unfortunately, economic considerations make it very difficult to maintain a reasonable quantity of fish in an area much less than an eighth of an acre — a medium sized back garden.

Small-scale farming has three main objectives. 1. To produce enough fish to supply a small family with at least one meal a week throughout the year, and to do this at reasonable cost. 2. To minimise running requirements (especially water flow). 3. To maintain the fish in good quality surroundings, so that their health and growth is not impaired.

Where a reasonable quantity of water is available, as from a small stream, fish can be reared very economically in a simple and easily built arrangement of tanks or dug-out ponds. However, where the supply is limited, it must be re-used. Fish pollute the environment in which they live, so recycling of water must also be accompanied by re-conditioning, involving the removal of harmful waste substances and the replenishment of oxygen. Reconditioning is usually achieved by passing contaminated water through a biological filter, which operates on the same principle as sewage works, where micro-organisms break down the biological wastes to simpler, harmless substances.

A recycling system is a closed microcosm, incorporating many of the natural cycles occurring in ponds and lakes. As such, its continued satisfactory operation depends on a delicate balance between many factors, and it is consequently more difficult to look after than an open system where the water is only used once. However, it is the only method of raising a significant quantity of fish with an insignificant supply of water.

Fish Farming Today

The meteoric rise in popularity of fish farming over the last fifty years has been linked with advances in aquatic biology and the search for alternative food sources, together with increasing pressure from leisure pursuits. Fish are produced not only for food, but for the extensive tropical and sport fish markets as well.

From virtually nothing at the end of the last century, fish culture has now grown to the point where it contributes 5 million tonnes of fish to the total world catch each year. This is nearly 6% of the annual global fish harvest, produced from a fraction of 1% of the world's waters. Despite the introduction of several new species, carp and carp-like fish still comprise a large proportion of farmed fish, especially in China, India and Indonesia. The common carp is the most popular fish in Europe, and its family includes the roach and the tench. Nor does aquaculture confine itself solely to fish. Other organisms are now being cultured and these include several bivalve molluscs (mainly mussels and oysters) and crustaceans (shrimps, prawns and lobsters), as well as a considerable tonnage of various types of seaweed. Next to carp, fishes like trout and salmon are the most commonly cultivated species, dominating fish farming in Northern Europe, Britain and the higher latitudes of North America.

Hot and Cold Water Fish

Trout and carp are examples of a distinction that is made in fish culture, between warm and cold water species. Trout and other salmonids are termed cold water species because they feed and reproduce at temperatures below 20°C, and cannot survive in warmer water. On the other hand, carp and warm water fishes prefer temperatures above 20°C, and some die or cannot reproduce in conditions colder than this. There are, of course, species with intermediate requirements, but most farmed fish fall into one or the other category.

The poor survival of cold water species at higher temperatures is related to their respiratory oxygen requirements. All fish rely on oxygen dissolved in the water for their respiration, and even under the most favourable conditions this is a very small amount. At higher temperatures, less oxygen can dissolve in the water, and the unfortunate fish can easily suffocate. This is a very critical factor in fish farming.

As well as these temperature requirements, the two groups tend to feed and reproduce slightly differently. Many of the cultivated cyprinids (carp) are omnivorous or phytophagous, whereas trout and salmon (salmonids) are exclusively carnivorous. Warm-water species also tend to exhibit a greater fecundity, with a corresponding reduction in egg size, compared with the cold-water fish.

Which Fish to Farm?

The desirable characteristics a fish should possess if it is to be suitable for commercial farming in semi-intensive earthen pond culture are:

1.   The fish species should be able to tolerate the pond conditions, in terms of both stocking density and environmental fluctuation, which may be temperature, water flow, water quality or whatever.

2.   They should grow quickly, on the natural food and/or any artificial food that may be distributed, and produce acceptable flesh.

3.   They should reproduce under the conditions of rearing, although not too readily, and the young should be sufficiently hardy to feed and survive adequately without too much attention.

4.   They should be resistant to disease and a certain amount of handling, and should be passive to facilitate harvesting.

In the small operation, where culture is carried out on an intensive scale, the first two considerations are most important.

No fish species can perfectly fulfill all the requirements listed above, but some are better than others. We have selected four types of freshwater fish which we think are most suitable for small scale farming. All of these are fairly easy to obtain at a reasonable price and are gastronomically acceptable! They also illustrate different methods of culture.

We have chosen rainbow trout, mirror carp, channel catfish and tilapia to describe in detail. Trout, and to a lesser extent carp, may be familiar as edible species in Britain, but channel catfish and tilapia are exotic, and rarely found on the fishmonger's slab. Both these species, together with rainbow trout, are cultured in the USA and are fairly popular; in fact rainbow trout as a regular meal is a far commoner sight in the USA than in Britain. *It would, however, be wise to taste any unfamiliar species before attempting to rear them* . . . . . .

Although all four species are available in the USA, channel cat-fish cannot be obtained in Britain and tilapia are only available as an aquarium fish. Accidental release of channel catfish into the wild in Britain could quite easily lead to this exotic species becoming established here, so their importation is justifiably prohibited. The species of tilapia we suggest farming are unlikely to overwinter in Britain, but their culture in outdoor ponds is also prohibited.

1 the four species of fish

Rainbow Trout

In Britain and the cooler parts of the USA, trout are undoubtedly the best fish for culture. They are the easiest species to keep from egg right through to adult, and are readily available and cheap to buy. They grow rapidly in cold water, which the other three species do not, and their flesh has a delicate flavour which is widely appreciated.

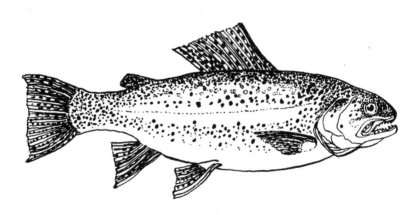

Fig. 1   **Rainbow Trout** (*Salmo gairdneri* ♂)

The biology of trout has been investigated in more detail than any other domesticated species and their culture requirements are well-known. They are tolerant of high density stocking and will take artificial food immediately after hatching. They mature sexually under most conditions of rearing and the eggs can be taken and fertilised externally by hand. The adults are also easy to prepare for the table and the dressing-out weight (the proportion of inedible parts of the fish, such as head and viscera) is not high.

On the other hand, they need a good supply of well-oxygenated water, which can be difficult to provide, especially in a pond, and they also require a diet rich in digestible protein. At certain stocking densities, aggressiveness can be a major problem, weakening the resistance of affected individuals to disease. This aggressiveness is enhanced when mature males are confined together, because of territorial behaviour.

Trout require the simplest type of recycling system for their culture and are marginally the cheapest to keep under these conditions. (Problems of aggression can be minimised by eating the fish before they become sexually mature!)

Mirror Carp

Mirror carp are a warm water species growing best at temperatures around 28°C. They show very rapid growth under the right conditions and can utilise a more varied and lower quality diet than rainbow trout while still growing quickly. They can also tolerate very high stocking densities, because they are docile and able to withstand lower dissolved oxygen levels than many other fish. This ability effectively means they can get by in a poorer quality environment than cold water species, especially as it is coupled with a resistance to other toxic elements. Carp are easily obtained and are usually only slightly more expensive than trout.

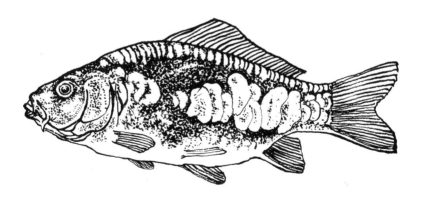

Fig. 2   **Mirror Carp** (*Cyprinus Carpio* ♂ or ♀)

Despite the fact that mirror carp prefer warm water they are not harmed by very cold conditions, although they become lethargic, stop eating and will consequently not grow. They can thus be overwintered in cold climates without much difficulty and are good fish for culture both in ponds and recycling systems. They have a relatively small head and a deep body, so there is less flesh wastage after dressing: this flesh is of good quality, finely textured and possessed of a distinctive flavour.

The major disadvantage of carp farming is their need for warm water. In Britain they will only grow for a few months of the year when the water temperature is high enough. It is not really feasible to heat a pond and even though recycling systems can be economically viable in this respect, heating pushes up the cost of producing the fish. Natural reproduction in ponds and recycling systems is difficult to achieve. To ensure spawning, special shallow ponds, termed Dubisch ponds, have to be constructed which both warm up quickly to the required temperature (at least 18°C) and provide the other biological stimuli necessary for natural spawning. In recycling systems, although the fish mature, they cannot release the eggs without interference and have to be given injections of a hormone preparation. Induced spawning, as this process is called, is expensive but worthwhile because of the large number of eggs (many thousands) that one female carp can produce; but the technique is very sophisticated and it is better to start with young fish and grow these up to an edible size.

Channel Catfish

The history of catfish culture in the southern United States is very short. Practised on a limited scale in the 1950's, it is now a large industry and it is fair to say that no other species has had its culture requirements investigated in comparable detail in so short a time.

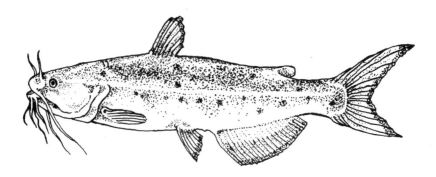

Fig. 3   Channel Catfish (*Ictalurus punctatus* ♂ or ♀)

Channel catfish are like carp in several ways. They are a warm-water fish, but their temperature demands are slightly lower (21—26°C). They are omnivorous and accept artificial diets without much trouble, so intensive culture techniques are well-established. In addition to possessing the ability to withstand high stocking densities, they can tolerate low winter temperatures and perform as well in ponds as recycling systems. Deep bodied, with rather bland flesh, they do not have as many fine bones as carp, so they lend themselves to processing quite readily.

They do need water with a high level of dissolved oxygen, being more like trout than carp in this respect, and this can be difficult to supply at higher water temperatures. They are excitable and sensitive to handling, which reduces their suitability for recycling systems where they may be constantly disturbed by the farmer. The head is fairly large and considered by some to be unsightly, which detracts from their table appeal to a certain extent.

Reproduction occurs in the Spring in the southern USA when water temperatures reach a suitable level, so ponds similar to the Dubisch type for carp are employed for the same reasons. Catfish do not reproduce in recycling systems, although they mature and can be induced to spawn with hormone injections like cyprinids. Though not as suitable as carp, catfish are a satisfactory species for intensive cultivation.

Tilapia

Tilapia have been something of an overnight sensation in fish farming. They have actually been exploited for some considerable time, but their potential as a farm fish was 'rediscovered' during, or just after, the Second World War. The Japanese occupation of Far Eastern countries with established fish culture industries (notably milkfish production) disrupted normal husbandry in many cases and ponds were allowed to fall into disrepair. After the troops withdrew, and life began to get back to normal, it was commonly found that ponds had been colonised by tilapia, especially the Java tilapia. The high productivity of the invaded ponds encouraged organised farming of tilapia, formerly considered an undesirable species, and numerous ponds were not returned to milkfish cultivation. Now, apart from their almost universal use on the African continent, virtually every developed country in the world has carried out experimental tilapia culture of some form.

These cichlid fishes have several attributes which make them ideal for aquaculture in warmer areas of the world. There are a wide variety of tilapia to choose from, to meet any farming situation, providing a huge gene pool for selective breeding. All show rapid growth and an ability to breed under the most diverse conditions; they are remarkably tolerant of high temperatures, low oxygen levels, overcrowding, varying salinities and generally atrocious environmental con-

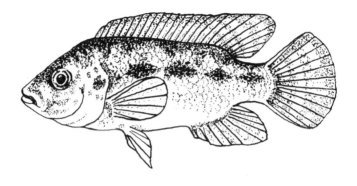

Fig. 4   Java Tilapia (*Sarotherodon mossambica* ♀)

ditions. They can be reared equally well in a reservoir or a drainage ditch. Tilapia are omnivorous or herbivorous, and can be fed on waste vegetable matter in some cases.

The breeding season for tilapia extends throughout the year provided water temperatures remain high. Apart from the bewildering choice that confronts the fish farmer and the inability of these fish to survive low temperatures, prolific reproduction constitutes their major disadvantage especially as a considerable proportion of any harvest is likely to be fish of an inedible size. One answer to this problem is to include a predator which selectively destroys the unwanted young among the tilapia population.

In temperate climates some form of heating has to be provided in order to sustain maximum growth and, possibly, to overwinter the

Fig. 5   Nile Tilapia (*Sarotherodon nilotica* ♀)

fish. Tilapia can easily grow to a satisfactory size in six months, so only a few brood fish need be overwintered unless it is desired to continue production throughout the year. Heating requirements can be minimised in this way, although continuity of supply can only be maintained in the winter months by preservation of the culled fish, either by freezing, salting or smoking.

Which species of tilapia to keep depends on a number of considerations. All are adaptable to ponds and recycling systems which can be kept warm, but it is important to choose a type which will feed and grow well on various kinds of vegetable refuse and cheap compounded diets, and is not too prolific. In practice this narrows the choice to the mouth-brooders which do not produce great numbers of eggs at a time. The Java tilapia is usually available from aquarist shops; although fairly expensive there is no need to pay out more than once for the fish as only a few mature fish are needed. It is predominantly a plankton eater but will feed on prepared diets, insect larvae, crustaceans and detritus. The Nile tilapia, which is more difficult to obtain, makes better use of leafy plant material than the Java tilapia and both species may be raised together if desired.

In Britain and the USA, the import of exotic species like tilapia is controlled by government, or state, regulations. These are really designed to protect natural waters from colonisation by foreign fish which may have disastrous consequences for the native ecology. Tilapia, of course, cannot survive for long in North American or European climates, unless the water is subject to thermal pollution, but it is important not to give them an opportunity to try.

NOTES ON FISH BIOLOGY

Before we look at the subject in depth there are some aspects of the biology of fish, important to the farmer, which should be understood because they govern the fish's behaviour in a given set of circumstances. Understanding feeding, digestion, respiration and excretion is particularly important.

The Digestive System

This is where the major input of a farm (the food supplied by the farmer) begins to be turned into output (flesh for consumption). The efficiency with which food is assimilated will vary but it is important to ensure that little of the distributed food is wasted. The food conversion coefficient describes the efficiency with which food is converted into flesh, being the ratio of the weight of the food eaten to the weight gain of the fish. This varies with the type of diet, the fish species, individual fish, temperature and a host of other factors which will be explained in the chapter dealing with nutrition.

A major distinction is evident between the digestive tracts of carnivorous and non-carnivorous fishes. Although fish have the same essential organs as all vertebrates, the intestines are relatively short when compared with those of land animals. Carnivorous fish have a well-defined stomach which is very extensible and allows them to gorge themselves with food. Most of the digestive processes occur here in an acid environment; fish such as trout are 'crammers' — they eat one big meal and then rest while they digest it. When distributing pelleted food to trout a feeding frenzy can occur, and after stimulation with a favoured food they will continue to eat diets which at other times they appear to regard as distasteful.

Omnivorous fish like carp are 'nibblers'; they often have soft mouths and tend to be discriminatory in their feeding habits in the wild. They have a relatively long intestine and a much-reduced or absent stomach. The absence of a stomach means that if gorging takes place, the intestine may become filled with food and partially digested matter voided before the fish has gained its full nutritional value. Carp are adapted to taking a small amount of food continuously throughout the day and, for this reason, it is better to feed them little and often, to ensure that assimilation is as complete as possible.

Fish are poikilothermic; they cannot maintain their body temperature at a level substantially different from their surroundings. Consequently, temperature has a profound effect on their metabolism. Increase in temperature causes a corresponding increase in basal metabolic rate, which is reflected in an increase in food consumption, activity and respiration.

Respiration

It has already been mentioned that fish depend on oxygen dissolved in the water for their breathing. Since oxygen is sparingly soluble this is always a small amount, and the respiratory structures of fish, the gills, have to be very efficient to compensate. Their structure allows the respiratory water to be brought into complete contact with the surfaces where gaseous exchange takes place. Typically 50—80% of the dissolved oxygen is removed from the water in a single passage across the gills a much higher efficiency than that obtained by our lungs — because of the special design of the blood supply.

Since the dividing line between no oxygen and complete saturation of the water is so small it is important to ensure that the water is well-oxygenated at all times, especially when keeping fish at elevated temperatures. The solution of oxygen in water occurs by direct diffusion of the gas into the liquid, and any increase in surface area of contact between the two will aid the diffusion process. Mechanical agitation, or spraying water under pressure onto or into a water body will improve oxygenation, as well as helping to drive off excess carbon dioxide.

Excretion

In addition to their function in respiration, the gills are also one of the main excretory routes of the fish. Ammonia is the predominant form of nitrogen eliminated by fish and some studies have shown that up to 80% of the total nitrogen waste products are in this form, the rest being largely urea passed with the urine. Unionised ammonia (NH_3) is by far the most toxic exretory product of fish, as in this form it can pass the tissue barrier. Ionised ammonia (NH_4^+) cannot do this, and is consequently less toxic. The formation of the ionised form is favoured by a decreasing pH, as the increased formation of hydrogen ions means more are available to combine with NH_3 to form NH_4^+. A decrease in pH from 8 to 7 results in a tenfold increase in the concentration of ionised ammonia, and an accompanying tenfold decrease in toxicity to the fish.

The action of the bacteria in a biological filter removes this ammonia but careful design is necessary to ensure that ammonia levels are kept to a minimum. A chronic level is one of the most serious problems affecting recycling systems and this will be dealt with in the chapter concerned with their upkeep.

2 ponds and pond construction

Ponds are likely to be of use to the farmer who is not restricted by the availability of water or space. Small ponds have the advantages of relatively inexpensive construction, low running costs and natural production of food for the fish. Small fish farms using ponds are the best means of raising fish for home consumption, although outdoor installations are limited to a certain extent by climate.

About Ponds

The use of natural free-standing ponds and lakes for keeping fish is the basis of the most ancient types of fish farming. However, most of the culture ponds in use today are in some degree artificial, being either man-made, or altered to suit his purposes. The construction, running and output of such ponds has been, and still is, a subject of much investigation.

Instructions for the management of natural ponds and lakes are beyond the scope of this book, for it is impossible to make generalisations about the best way to look after a particular pond since every pond is unique due to variations in size, shape, climate and ecology. However, we can provide guidelines for the construction and maintenance of artificial ponds where a reasonable degree of control over the environment can be exercised. The management of natural ponds really falls into the extensive category since little or no improving measures are taken to increase the natural maximum number of fish that the water body will support.

There are many factors to be considered when designing and operating ponds, and we have attempted to set out this section in the order in which questions might occur. It should be borne in mind that pond building in Britain and the USA has associated legal requirements regulating construction, water extraction and disposal. Although we have relegated these to a specific chapter the appropriate authorities must have given their approval before the commencement of any work.

The Construction of Ponds

The first requirement for a pond is water — enough of the right kind and in the right place. The volume of water needed will depend on the type, size and intensity of use of the pond, as well as the species farmed. All fish need good quality water containing adequate dissolved oxygen, free of substances detrimental to them and of a suitable temperature. It is also obviously no use trying to build a pond where there is no water for miles around.

The water supply usually comes from one of three sources: 1) Spring or borehole water is often the best, because it is likely to be pure and clean, with a stable year-round flow. If a good source of ground water is near then you are very lucky. 2) The most common water supply is from a water course, such as a stream or river. These may contain natural stocks of fish, so there is the possibility of disease; smaller streams frequently have seasonal variation in flow, and may dry up completely during the summer months. It is important to establish what is termed the 'dry year flow' for such sources, so as to know what minimum flow to expect. The frequency of flooding must also be taken into consideration, when problems like siltation will occur. 3) Surface runoff; when ponds are filled with periodic flows after rain. This is the least suitable supply, there is little predictability and consequently poor scope for any intensive system of husbandry.

Smaller ponds will be subjected to rapid fluctuations in water level and temperature, amongst other things. This will stress the fish and make a planned schedule of husbandry very difficult. A pond with a water flow which at least compensates for water losses and maintains a steady level throughout the year is therefore preferable. A higher water flow will increase the output of the pond and allow more flexibility of use.

The need for a water flow into a pond is firstly to meet the oxygen demands of the fish and secondly, to remove their waste products before they accumulate to harmful levels. In ponds without a water flow, or one that just keeps pace with evaporation and seepage, the number of fish that can be stocked depends on the type of fish and the available oxygen. For cold water species, like salmonids, this number will be smaller than for coarse fish. The amount of oxygen in the water can be increased by various means without an increased flow, but toxic metabolites may then become limiting.

Given a water supply with a reasonable flow the next step is to check the quality of the water. Is it turbid or clear? Water with a heavy load of mud or detritus is not good — it will interfere with the fish's breathing and settle out on the bottom of the pond, blocking drainage channels and necessitating regular dredging or draining, or both. A thick mud also encourages the growth of weed.

The chemical characteristics of the water are important. The first things to check are the pH and the dissolved oxygen. Water with a low pH (acid) value is usually low in dissolved salts and has no buffering capacity, which is the ability of the water to oppose changes in pH. Acid waters do not encourage the growth of beneficial plants which make a pond fertile, so the proportion of natural food available to the fish will be low. A very low pH is bad for the fish themselves. Water with a neutral or slightly alkaline reaction is ideal. A good buffering capacity keeps the pH stable and promotes the growth of beneficial plants.

Dissolved oxygen levels should be as high as possible, near saturation at the particular temperature of the water. Low dissolved oxygen readings imply either that the water is still and has not been in sufficient contact with the air, or more seriously that there is a high proportion of organic substances in the water that are tending to remove the oxygen. The Biochemical Oxygen Demand (BOD) is a measure of the oxygen removing capacity of substances in the water. For instance, sewage has a high BOD because the large numbers of micro-organisms that are breaking down the waste organic matter in the sewage require oxygen to do so. Water with a BOD exceeding 3mg per litre is not suitable for intensive fish culture.

The amount of water that will be required is dependent on three main factors. These are:
(1) The type of fish stocked.
(2) The intensity of use of the pond.
(3) The size of the pond.

The greatest water flow will be needed for intensive culture of salmonids like rainbow trout, and it has been reported that 1 litre per minute per kilogram of fish weight at a temperature of $15^{\circ}C$ is a good working approximation for estimating the potential of a water supply.

The Pond

Basically, there are two types of pond; those built on the ground and those built in it. In the first type water is retained by a dam, dyke or embankment of some sort, usually at a level above the surrounding ground. In the second it is allowed to collect in a depression or excavation, the water surface being at or below ground level. The first type is preferred in practice because it can be easily drained, facilitating harvesting of the fish crop and maintenance of the pond. Where the topography is suitable ponds may be made by a single dam across a water course, similar to flooded valley reservoirs.

In either case, the soil has to be suitable for pond construction unless it is intended to use concrete or plastic liners. A very porous material like sand will never retain water, unless it is underlain by

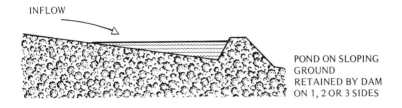

INFLOW

POND ON SLOPING
GROUND
RETAINED BY DAM
ON 1, 2 OR 3 SIDES

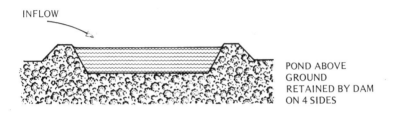

INFLOW

POND ABOVE
GROUND
RETAINED BY DAM
ON 4 SIDES

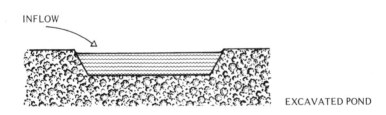

INFLOW

EXCAVATED POND

Fig. 6   **Types of Pond**

impervious rocks. Most soils with a percentage of clay will tamp down
and hold water, but it is best to seek advice on this subject, or at least
to carry out some experiments before trying to build a pond.

Size, Shape and Depth
Fish farming ponds are all sizes, from five square yards to five square
miles! It is generally reckoned that for small ponds between one and
five ares is most suitable. One are is 100 square metres or one-fortieth
of an acre. A pond of one are in extent is thought to be the minimum
worthwile for intensive farming, whilst above five ares is too large for
one or two people to manage on a part-time basis.

17

When buying in small fish and keeping a stock of all sizes, it is better to have several ponds in order to keep the size groups separate (see below).

Smaller ponds, as well as being more manageable, can be harvested quickly, are less subject to wind erosion and can be treated more effectively and economically should diseases occur. If a pond is constructed on ground level, with the water retained by an embankment, then the most useful shape is a square. With oblong or irregular ponds, a greater length of dyke will be required to give the same surface area as a square pond. For example, a square pond with a surface area of one are would need 40 metres of walling, while an oblong pond of the same area with a width of 5 metres would need 50 metres. It will not always be possible to determine the shape of a pond in advance, of course, but some thought should be given to the most practical shape. Circular ponds may seem more traditional, but rectangular ponds are more accessible and space saving.

Deep ponds are not utilised by fish completely. With a water depth of more than 2 metres temperature and dissolved oxygen stratification can occur. The bottom water is not mixed with the surface layers and for parts of the year what is termed a thermocline may develop. A thermocline is really a boundary between water levels at different temperatures and occurs because of one of the peculiar properties of water. Water at $4^{o}C$ is at its least volume and maximum density, so that it will sink to the bottom of the pond. Warmer water will float on top of this cold, dense water, which is often deficient in dissolved oxygen, and distinct temperature zones will have been set up. Fish will not penetrate this cooler water under normal circumstances, so a proportion of the pond is not being used. Nutrients which in shallower water would be recycled through the pond from the bottom mud remain locked up there, reducing the overall productivity.

Shallower water prevents the establishment of a thermocline, and the optimum depth is between one and 1.3 metres. This is too deep for over-heating in summer, too deep for submerged vegetation to invade the edges of the pond, but shallow enough to encourage maximum productivity and promote warming to desirable temperatures. In temperate countries, when the summer does finally arrive, this last point is especially important in order that warm water species like carp have as long a growing season as possible. Unfortunately relatively rapid summer warming also means rapid winter cooling. During winter the temperature of a shallow pond falls quickly, so that it is common practice in Europe to provide deeper wintering ponds for species like carp. These have a depth of between 2 and 3 metres, so that freezing of the surface water will not endanger the fish.

Layout
There is no general rule for planning ponds for it is not always possible

to determine in advance what shape they will take. For a series of ponds, however, there are several points to be considered. If the water supply to the pond(s) is more than adequate, or liable to flood, it is a good idea to have a diversion channel at one side to carry away surplus water. Consecutive flow (i.e. the outflow of one pond serving as the inflow to the next) should be avoided if possible, otherwise the waste from one will be carried into the next. This is bad for the fish, for the environment in successive ponds will gradually deteriorate. Should disease occur in one it will be transmitted to all the others. Water should be supplied to each pond individually from a central or lateral channel and the outflow carried away separately.

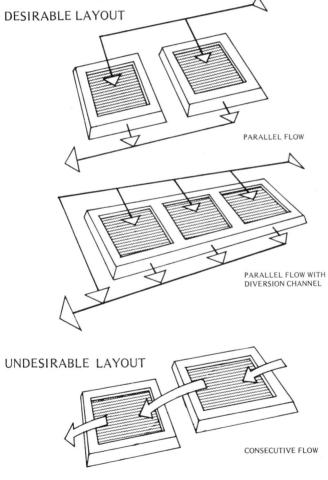

DESIRABLE LAYOUT

PARALLEL FLOW

PARALLEL FLOW WITH
DIVERSION CHANNEL

UNDESIRABLE LAYOUT

CONSECUTIVE FLOW

Fig. 7 **Pond Layout**

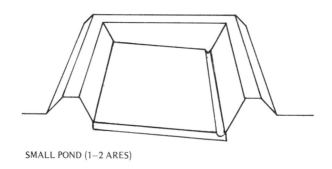

SMALL POND (1–2 ARES)

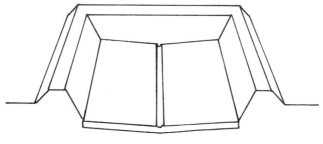

SMALL POND (1–2 ARES)

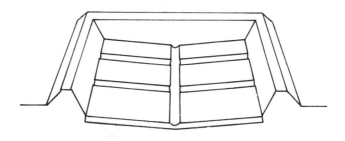

LARGE POND (OVER 2 ARES)

Fig. 8 **Pond Drainage**

As previously mentioned, a pond that can be drained will be easier to manage and more productive than a pond kept permanently under water. It is best to arrange gravity drainage where possible. Accordingly, some attention should be given to the pond bottom in order to facilitate rapid and complete drainage. The drying-out of a pond bottom is beneficial for it allows sun and air to get at the mud.

Drainage is assisted by a system of shallow drainage ditches dug in the pond bottom converging at the water outlet, which must itself be lower than the lowest point in the pond. The whole pond bottom should also slope gently towards this outlet point with a fall of about 1 metre in a thousand. Unless the pond bottom is particularly firm a slope much greater than this will cause turbidity and erosion during draining and fish collecting in the ditches may drown in the muddied water.

Lateral drainage ditches may be dispensed with in ponds of 1—2 ares, only a single central drainage channel being necessary provided the pond bottom slopes in to this. Larger ponds should have a fishbone shaped network of channels spaced 8—15 metres apart. Alternatively, lateral main drainage channels may be used where the pond bottom slopes to one or either side, with secondary channels again in the larger ponds. Care should be taken in the initial preparation of the bottom to eliminate pockets and hollows that would remain full of water when the pond was dried. For this reason it is best to carry out some rudimentary levelling of the site before construction begins, especially when natural depressions are going to be flooded by a dyke across a water course.

Rough levelling can be effected by stakes, driven into the ground, joined with pieces of string at the height of the intended water level. The strings can then be levelled with a spirit level in the same way that a bricklayer gauges his courses. More accurate surveying could be done with a theodolite.

The drainage ditches themselves should be about 40cm deep and 75cm wide in the case of a main channel and 20—30cm deep in the lateral channels. Larger ponds require proportionately larger channels. It is a good idea to line the main drainage channel with stones or concrete to prevent erosion and to widen it somewhat before the outflow of the pond so that the fish collect in this part. This will be unnecessary in a small pond, but is worthwhile in ponds over 4 ares. Such a collecting basin should not be deeper than the outflow channel, for it should be drained dry with the rest of the pond after the fish are caught. All ditches will need re-digging or cleaning out after a draining for they quickly become silted up and useless.

Plumbing

Getting water to and from the ponds can be a headache, especially when utilising a surface water supply such as a stream or river. Springs and artesian boreholes will usually have sufficient water pressure to allow ponds to be sited above ground, simplifying supply and drainage, but low head sites (eg. a stream flowing through flat meadow land) present difficulties. If possible, supply water should have some back-pressure so that inflow can be sited above the pond water level, thereby promoting aeration and preventing fish getting in or out of the pond.

If a stream has a very low fall, it will be too expensive to run lengths of piping or conduit needed to carry water from an upstream site. Electric pumping is too expensive for small fish ponds unless it is employed for domestic purposes by necessity, and provides an otherwise wasted excess. Wind pumps are also unsuitable, for the very time when water is needed most, during hot weather, is usually the time when wind pumps are becalmed. Because of their high stocking density, all small ponds need a continuous supply of water; intermittent supplies are only suitable for large ponds.

One possible means of overcoming the disadvantages of a low head site is to use a waterwheel or a hydraulic ram. In streams with a relatively large flow, a water wheel could be used to lift water into a supply channel, although the energetics involved means that only a small proportion of the stream flow can be diverted in this way, and a fairly large wheel would be needed to meet the requirements of our small ponds. For the same reason, a large hydraulic ram would be necessary.

Dykes and Digging

After the site is chosen and the design of the pond(s) decided, comes the actual work. All ponds will require a certain amount of excavation, to throw up an embankment or dyke. With smaller ponds this earth will have to be removed from the whole area of the pond bottom so that a minimal lowering of ground level occurs, otherwise, at a later stage, problems will be encountered with drainage. Larger ponds can have dykes built with earth from a borrow pit at the foot of the dyke, which can then act as a drainage ditch, soakaway or both.

The dyke of drainable ponds is their most important feature. If it is not built carefully and well, then the pond will not function for very long. Leaky dykes are virtually impossible to seal effectively and 'a leak means weak'; constant seepage will undermine the banks and eventually cause collapse of the dyke altogether.

Dykes are usually made of rammed earth, a wide variety of topsoils compacting to give the desired qualities of water tightness and strength. A percentage of clay varying from 20% to 60% would be satisfactory, with the best dyke material consisting of about 60% clay, 40% sand. Heavy or pure clay is very difficult to work and subject to cracking in dry weather; it should really only be used as a core inside the dyke where it is necessary to key in to watertight foundations. Soil that contains a lot of humus, such as rich loams and peat, will reduce the strength of a dyke because they will tend to decompose and slump, or form channels through the dyke. Pebbles, if they are too numerous, will also create channels through the dyke, and it may prove necessary to sieve all the soil as successive layers of the dyke are being built.

Earth dams should be built in successive layers about 30cm thick, each one being rammed down hard with a heavy wooden pole, or by the weight of a tractor, before the next is added. No matter how good the compaction, dykes will tend to sink a little as they settle down, and

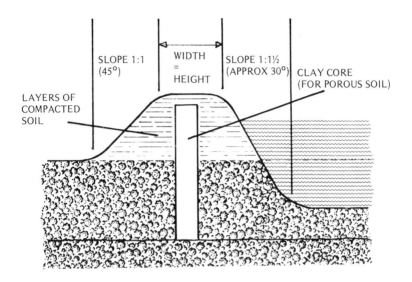

Fig. 9 **Cross Section of Dyke**

therefore the total height of the newly completed dyke should be about 20% higher than desired. All the earth used in construction should be damp, to aid in compaction, and very dry soils should be moistened before working. Key cores for waterproofing dykes made of porous earth should be about 45cm thick. There is no need to sink the whole dyke to the level of the waterproof ground; it is only necessary to dig a narrow trench and fill this with clay. The dyke may be built on top of the ground surface provided this is firm and stable.

It is usually recommended that dykes should be as thick at the top as they are high and never less than 1 metre. Their height should be sufficient to exceed the proposed water level by at least 30cm or more, depending on the size of the pond, exposure and susceptibility to flooding.

The pond side of a dyke should have a slope of between 1:1½ for small ponds (approximately 2–6 ares) and 1:2 or 3 for larger ponds. The outside wall should have a slope of about 1:1 or 1½. A dyke 2 metres high, and 1 metre wide at its apex, would therefore be 5 metres

23

wide at its base. Very small ponds (1—2 ares) would not need to be quite so over-engineered, and a dyke height of just over 1 metre, apex width of 0.5 metre and base width of 2 metres would be adequate.

The finished rammed earth dam should be sown with grass seed to consolidate the surface material and prevent erosion, any self-seeded trees or shrubs should be removed for their roots can break up the dyke. Although overhanging vegetation can often supply food, in the form of insect larvae and grubs, shading of a pond in this way will both retard warming in summer and damage the banks. Windbreaks and shade are useful in trout ponds where the water may need to be kept cool during summer, but are not needed in coarse fish rearing ponds.

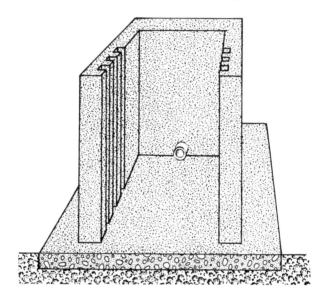

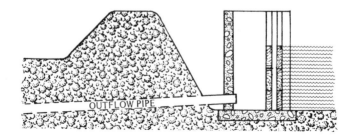

OUTFLOW PIPE

Fig. 10 **The Monk and its Relationship to the Dyke**

The device for regulating the outflow and water level in ponds, known as a 'monk', has now gained almost universal acceptance on fish farms throughout the world. It consists of a U shaped concrete or wooden structure set next to the dyke wall at the outlet point. The open end of the U is directed toward the water of the pond and is blocked off by a number of removable boards. The outflowing water runs over the top of these boards into the monk and is evacuated through a pipe at its base. By removing or adding boards across the mouth of the monk the water level in the pond can be regulated or the pond drained completely. Often two grooves for two series of planks are built into the monk, the space between these boards is filled with clay to ensure the water flows across their tops only. Water can be evacuated from the bottom of a pond as well by leaving a gap at the bottom of the first set of boards and regulating the water level by the second set. This is useful in larger, deeper ponds where the cold bottom water caused by a thermocline can be removed without interfering with the warm productive upper layers.

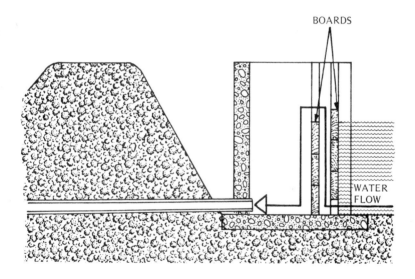

Fig. 11 Draining the Pond from the Bottom

A screen is provided in front of the boards to prevent the escape of fish, the size of mesh depending on the size of fish in the pond. Screens require regular cleaning because they quickly get blocked with leaves and twigs that blow or get washed into the pond. The screen must be higher than the water level (ie. higher than the topmost board in the monk) to stop larger fish from jumping over.

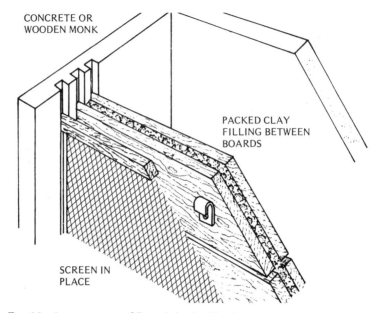

Fig. 12 **Arrangement of Boards in the Monk**

CONCRETE OR
WOODEN MONK

PACKED CLAY
FILLING BETWEEN
BOARDS

SCREEN IN
PLACE

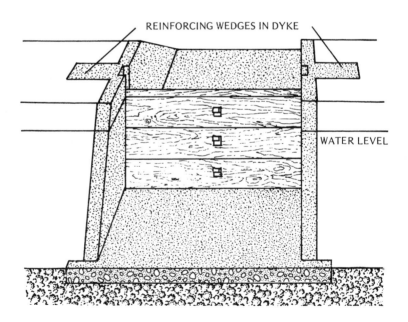

Fig. 13 **The Sluice**

REINFORCING WEDGES IN DYKE

WATER LEVEL

Apart from the monk, the other most popular water regulating device is the sluice. This works on the same principle as the monk, with removable boards, but it involves a breach through the dyke which may weaken it if suitable reinforcement is not included. A monk, apart from being easier to construct, avoids this problem.

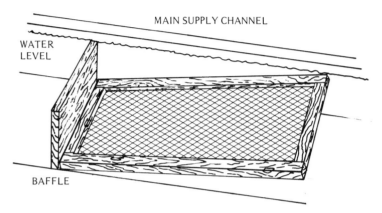

Fig. 14 **Sunken Horizontal Screen**

The water inflow to a pond must also be fish proof. This can be effected either by placing the inflow well above the surface of the water, which incidentally improves oxygenation of the water by splashing, or by fitting a screen. The most suitable type of screen for the inflow is horizontal and sunk beneath the surface of the water. This type tends to clog less frequently and is very effective in preventing the escape of fish, but does require construction of a concrete inflow

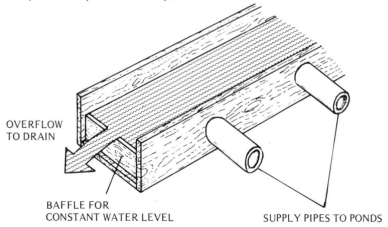

Fig. 15 **Wooden Supply Channel**

channel to give sufficient water depth to submerge the screen. Where water is supplied by a water course and may contain wild species, the horizontal screen is the best for stopping accidental introduction of these fish into the pond. In a pond containing small fry such an introduction could be disastrous if the wild fish were of a predatory species.

Water inflow must be controllable to avoid excess water flow in times of flood and to save or shut off the supply when the pond is understocked or drained. Control can be effected by several devices. Where a series of ponds are supplied from a central channel, water can be led off into the ponds by a miniature vertical screw sluice or an overflow weir similar to the monk. A sunken screen should be placed at either end of the central supply channel, in which a constant level of water should be maintained by overflow wiers at either end, particularly if there is any risk of fish escaping from the ponds. A piped water supply is simply regulated by a tap.

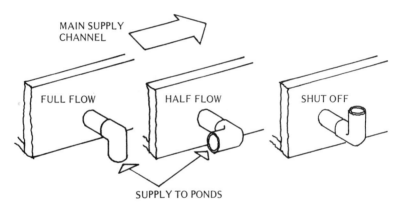

Fig. 16 **Inflow Regulation**

The Small Scale Fish Pond
We will now consider the type of pond suitable for each of our four fish species in turn. The greatest detail will be found in the section concerned with the husbandry of carp for they are representative of the techniques used in the farming of a large number of other warm water fish species.

3 pond culture of rainbow trout

Edible size rainbow trout weigh between 150 and 250g, which is achieved after about eighteen months growth under favourable conditions. To meet our production target of enough fish to supply a small family with one meal a week throughout the year, a small fish farm must be capable of supplying approximately 50kg of trout per year, or 200 fish each weighing 250g. This means a stock of smaller trout must be kept at the same time to maintain continuity of supply. It is best to have three separate age/weight classes and, consequently, three ponds or tanks.

Semi-intensive Culture
Here we are concerned with the rearing of trout in earthen ponds, using fertilisation to increase natural productivity, and practising some form of supplemental feeding. The size of the ponds required depends upon what proportion of the total diet is composed of natural food. Where earthen ponds are employed, we have decided to recommend larger ponds than strictly necessary, so as to increase the contribution of natural food. Minimum volume rearing (i.e. highest density of stocking) is described for intensive farming in circular tanks.

Construction of the Ponds
There should be three main growing ponds, covering in total about 2.5 ares (250 square metres). In addition a small holding pond, or tank, for the edible sized fish, around 5 square metres, would prove useful. All three main ponds should have a separate water supply, and a parallel arrangement is usually the most convenient.

First Pond This is for holding the smallest fish (fingerlings) and should be rectangular in shape, 50 square metres in area, and 0.75–1 metre deep. This pond should be stocked in March to April of each year with

Fig. 17 **Arrangement of Trout Ponds with Shade**

300 6–8cm fish. These will each weigh between 4.5–5g, and be about four to five months old. At this stage they will be well accustomed to an artificial diet and there will be no problems with feeding. The target weight for these fish at the end of the year is approximately 70g, when they will be 20cm long. The fingerlings should be removed from the first pond after six months and transplanted to the second rearing pond. The first pond is then drained and kept dry over the winter.

Second Pond This should be larger, roughly 1 are in extent. The fingerlings are transferred to this as soon as they reach an average weight of 30g, or 15cm length. Here they remain until the end of the year, or until they achieve the first year's growth target. They are then transferred to the third rearing pond.

Third Pond This pond should be the same size as the second, and is used for growing the table sized fish. Prior to stocking with fresh fish from the second pond, the remaining large trout should preferably be removed to a small holding pond, where they are kept until consumed. It is important to try and maintain the size distribution in any one pond as uniformly as possible. Trout are carnivorous and the smaller

30

individuals will be harassed. They will certainly lose their tails and some may die. In any case, mauled fish will lose some of their table appeal, be unhealthy and consequently not grow as fast as their aggressors. This poor growth is more marked when artificial food is distributed for they will be unable to compete successfully for their ration. As soon as the fish in the holding tank are used up cropping of the third main pond should begin. The larger of the fish in this pond, which should be about 150g after three months, are culled for eating. In this way a continuous supply of fish is available throughout the year.

The water flow to the first pond should at first be 1—2 litres per minute over and above that needed to meet evaporation and seepage losses, gradually increasing, over the six month occupation period, to 3—5 litres per minute. This serves to meet the oxygen requirements of the fish and to keep down the temperature. To this end, the other two rearing ponds should be made slightly deeper than is necessary for warm water species, about 1.3 to 1.5 metres. To avoid stress among the smaller fish, which are always kept in the shallowest pond throughout the warmest months of the year in temperate climates, the water temperature should not be allowed to rise much above $18^{\circ}C$. Temperatures of $15^{\circ}C$, however, are optimal for growth and this is the temperature to aim for in all the ponds for as long as possible.

Following the guidelines for pond construction outlined earlier, all three ponds should be made by throwing up an earth embankment. The soil for this is taken from the whole area of the pond, so that drainage levels are convenient. Inflow and outflow points in the first pond are best protected with 2mm mesh plastic netting, to prevent escapes. A monk for this size of pond is unnecessary and there are several alternatives. The most suitable is probably a plastic stand pipe surrounded by a larger piece of pipe covered by plastic netting at its base. This will regulate the water level at the desired height and draw off water from the bottom of the pond. All screens require daily attention if they are not to become clogged. Draining with this arrangement is easily effected by removing the centre pipe, if plastic push-together fittings are used.

Water flow in the second pond should begin at 3--4 litres per minute and be increased to about 8 litres per minute over the six months. The third pond should start with 8 litres per minute, increasing to 10 litres per minute after three months. This may gradually be reduced to 5—6 litres per minute over the next three months, as fish are culled for eating. The peak requirements of the small fish farm will be in the region of 40 litres per minute, if losses due to evaporation and seepage are not too great, and this value should easily be met by a small water course.

Water inlets are best set 50cm or so above the surface of the pond, to increase aeration. The water can be allowed to fall over a horizontal plate, causing it to fall in a sheet into the pond, to promote aeration yet

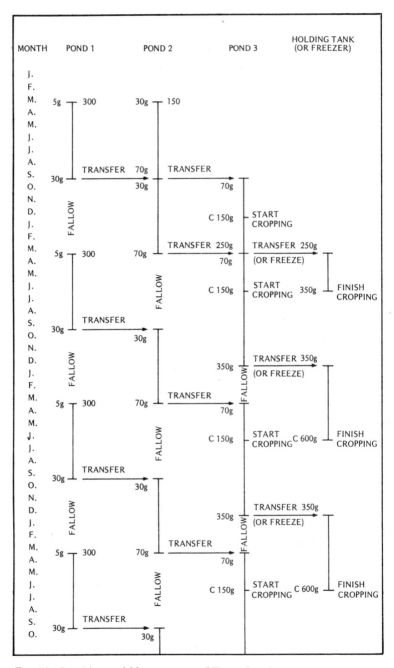

Fig. 18 **Stocking and Management of Trout Ponds**

further. It should be borne in mind that the inflow rates shown above may not be sufficient in very warm weather and should be increased if the fish show any signs of stress. After a little experience of keeping and handling fish, the culturist can quickly spot any signs of distress in his fish. Symptoms of discomfort due to oxygen lack or too high a temperature are usually rapid respiration and lethargy; suffocating fish will tend to lie near the surface in an attempt to find better quality water, or on the bottom if the temperature is too high. The symptoms due to various diseases are different and require a good deal more experience to identify.

Outflow from the two main ponds should be through a monk, and this must be screened with 1cm mesh in the second, intermediate size fingerling pond. Instead of a full screen in the third pond, the top board of the monk can be replaced with a 2cm mesh screen to permit easier cleaning.

The husbandry schedule shown in fig. 18 is designed to provide edible fish over a twelve month period, beginning 15 months after first stocking, and ending after 27 months.

New ponds freshly put under water tend to be more productive than older ponds because the soil gradually loses its mineral elements to the water. To bring the farm 'on-stream' more rapidly therefore, we suggest that the second pond is initially stocked with half the normal quantity of 30g, one year old fish at the same time as the first pond. Cropping can then commence after 9 months instead of 15, and will end in six months as the smallest trout reach an edible size.

By juggling the fully grown fish around, it is possible to dispense with the holding pond, but this will reduce the fallow periods of the other ponds. For example, if there is access to a freezer, edible fish removed from pond 3 in December to January could be held in pond 1 for three months, until this was due to be stocked with fresh fish. The remainder could then be killed and frozen for three months until the next crop of fish reached an edible size. The maximum storage time for oily fish like trout at $-18^{\circ}C$ is usually recommended as three months by most freezer manufacturers. Freezing large fish represents a considerable saving of supplementary food over three months, but using pond 1 as a temporary storage pond for the edible fish immediately before it is stocked with fingerlings increases the risk of disease transmission between the ponds. At least three dry months are desirable for all the ponds, for this will increase the natural productivity and ensure no predators or parasites survive to the next stocking.

The amount of supplementary feed that needs to be distributed to each pond throughout the eighteen months growing period is quite difficult to calculate because there are a number of factors to be taken into account. These are:

(1) The natural productivity of the pond.

(2) The increase in natural productivity brought about by fertilisation, if any.

(3) The growth of the fish.

(4) The food conversion.

(5) Mortality and culling (i.e. the number of fish to be fed at any one time).

Natural Productivity

The natural productivity of a pond is the sum total of all the life in that pond and may be quantitatively measured by weight, often referred to as the biomass. Some sort of evaluation of this biomass is useful for formulating a working plan for a particular pond, but it must be remembered that the fish can only use a part of the total biomass.

Ecological interrelations in pond productivity are not sufficiently understood to provide a simple and reliable method for accurately establishing natural pond productivity, but empirical models have been designed to give reasonable approximations. The most important of these is the Léger — Huet formula. It relies on careful observation of the biology of the pond and a subjective assessment of the productivity potential. The accuracy of this assessment really depends on experience and a good knowledge of freshwater biology. We cannot go into details here but readers should consult Huet's 'Textbook of Fish Culture' for the information.

One way to assess natural productivity is to stock a few fish in a pond and see how well they grow in a season. The amount of food they would have needed to be given to cause this growth is then a good guide to the natural food available each year. Natural productivity in small ponds will contribute only a very small part of the total food needed, but it is still worthwhile making this as great as possible by arranging good pond conditions. The quantity of useful food naturally produced in a pond is dependent on the quantity and quality of plant life, both living and dead, which feeds and shelters the microfauna and flora which in turn will eventually feed the fish. The desirable vegetation for a pond will depend to some extent on its use and determining factors are:

(1) *Temperature* which influences the development of aquatic microorganisms as well as directly influencing the growth, reproduction, respiration and nutrition of the fish.

(2) *Light* is essential for photosynthesis, as well as indirectly for heating, so that productivity will be reduced in shaded conditions. The *turbidity* of the water also plays a role in light transmission, acting as a filter for the sunlight; greenish or blueish waters indicate healthy phytoplankton growth, and are productive. Brown and yellow waters are often acid and biologically sterile.

(3) An undisturbed pond bottom is necessary for the development of a rich organic mud in which nutritive organisms become established.

Decomposition of organic wastes occurs here and inorganic nutrients are recycled to the rest of the water body. The chemical characteristics of the pond must be such that there are adequate supplies of mineral elements like calcium, nitrogen, phosphorous and potassium. The pH is a good reflector of the state of the pond, low (acid) values usually signifying low productivity. The best pH is about 7.5 to 8, slightly alkaline, with a good carbonate content, which helps to maintain constant pH. Defects in pH, and paucity of mineral nutrients can be corrected by liming and fertilisation. The pH should be corrected before placing any pond under water.

Fertilisation

Phosphorous, potassium and nitrogen are the three most important basic elements for fertilisation and they are usually found in ponds in small quantities, especially phosphorous.

The most important action of fertilisers is on the bottom mud of the pond, which in decomposing releases nutrients a little at a time to the flora and fauna feeding off it. Fertilisers applied to the pond are absorbed by the mud and released gradually as they are needed. Fertilisation therefore represents the most economical and long-term way of increasing pond productivity.

Before addition of any type of fertiliser to a pond, whether inorganic or organic, the chemical characteristics of the water and the pond bottom must be known. Both must be slightly alkaline and the bottom mud should be no more than 10cm deep, and composed of a fine detritus without undecomposed plant material. Any acidity may be corrected by addition of lime, as powdered limestone or quicklime. As in conventional agriculture, liming has several beneficial effects. It helps form a suitable crumb structure, which aids decomposition processes in the mud, and provides a reserve of carbon dioxide which combats any change in pH and helps assimilation by plants. It also brings about precipitation of excess organic matter in the water and destroys harmful parasites of the fish.

Lime is best applied to the ponds before they are put under water for the growing season and as a preliminary treatment before any fertilisation. Inorganic fertilisers are also best applied at this time. The type and amount of lime to be distributed depends on its purpose; powdered limestone is used for correcting a pH deficit, while quicklime because of its caustic properties, is generally used for disinfection. For general improvement purposes powdered limestone is to be preferred, evenly distributed at 4—8kg per are. Quicklime has twice the efficacy of limestone and should consequently be used in half the quantity. For correction of a pH deficit in the soil and water, the quantities required vary considerably according to the degree of acidity and the nature of the soil. It would be wise to seek advice on this point.

The Growth of the Fish

As the trout in each of the three ponds (and the holding tank) grow, the amount of supplementary feed to be distributed will have to increase. A sample of fish should be taken from each pond at weekly intervals and weighed. If a careful record of mortalities is kept, the number of fish in the pond will be known and the approximate total weight can be calculated from the sample. The amount of food required can then be adjusted at weekly intervals to meet the needs of the growing fish.

The Food Conversion

As was explained in the introduction, the food conversion is the ratio of the food fed to the weight gain of the fish. For example, a food conversion ratio of 2 would mean that for every kg of fish weight gained, 2kg of feed would have to be consumed. The food conversion is affected by a host of factors, such as temperature, metabolic energy expenditure, level of toxins like ammonia in the water, and type of food. With a reasonable natural productivity, it should be possible to maintain the food conversion ratio at 2.

The Number of Fish

An accurate and updated record must be kept of mortalities and fish removed for eating. This is most important for the fish that have reached an edible size in the third pond and the holding tank, for not only will their numbers be fluctuating the most rapidly, but they will be consuming the greatest weight of supplemental food. Each time fish are removed they should be weighed and the weight noted down. The daily ration for the remaining fish can then be altered accordingly.

We are now in a position to show how the amount of supplementary food needed can be calculated. Because the natural productivity of a pond will be peculiar to that pond, we will assume no contribution from natural food. When constructing backyard ponds, whether for trout, carp, channel catfish or tilapias, some effort should be made to assess the natural productivity and take it into account when working out the amount of food to distribute.

Supplementary Food

Trout need artificial rations containing substantial quantities of protein, and these are expensive. Any factor which increases the efficiency with which these are utilised for growth is of value, for it will reduce the quantity of feed required, and thus the cost. Although a smallholder or farmer may have access to a regular supply of good quality protein, such as offal, with which to formulate home-made supplementary rations, for most prospective fish farmers we would recommend the use of one of the commercial trout foods. In fish farming, as with most forms of intensive animal husbandry, the cost of feed represents the largest portion of all recurring costs.

The quantity of supplemental feed required for the smallest fish over their six month growing period will be 7.65kg (the growth target) multiplied by the food conversion ratio. This we have assumed as two making the total of supplemental feed needed 15.3kg.

For the other two ponds, calculation of the supplementary feed required is complicated by the degree of mortality encountered and the rate at which fish are removed for eating. We have allowed for a total loss of 30% (excluding the culled fish) throughout the growing period of eighteen months, for it will be recalled that our original aim was to produce approximately 200 edible sized trout of 250g each. The normal losses expected during extensive rearing of trout for the table are 50% for the first year, and 10% thereafter. Because of the much greater degree of control over the whole rearing process in the small ponds, natural mortality should not exceed 10% per year unless an accident occurs.

The growth target for the individual fish in the second pond is 70g, from an initial stocking weight of 30g. With an accurate record of mortalities, the corrected total of supplemental food can be easily calculated. It is not worth compensating for the deaths of one or two small fish, but as soon as the trout reach an individual weight of 20g, much more care should be taken. If too much food is distributed at one time, the trout will not be able to eat it all before it sinks to the bottom where it will be wasted. This is true for all age groups although there will always be a fairly high proportion of wastage with very small fish. This problem has been alleviated to some extent by the development of floating pelleted foods, some of which remain water stable for several hours.

In the third pond, fish will be removed for eating after the third month from stocking or whenever they reach an individual weight of 150g, at an average rate of four per week. The total supplementary food will be reduced progressively over the next nine months.

The Weekly Ration

Pond 1 In a suitable environment the growth of a fish will be continuous and will not take place by sudden increases at irregular intervals. The rate of growth of a fish is expressed as the number of units by which its weight increases divided by the amount of time that elapses while this weight increase is taking place. If this increase in weight is a constant proportion of the total body weight in unit time, it follows that the rate of growth as defined above will continuously increase with time. A 50g fish increasing in weight by 1% of its body weight per day will put on more weight per day than a 20g fish growing at the same rate. As a fish gets larger, so the net amount of weight it gains each day increases. Plotting the daily increase in weight against time, we get the J-shaped curve shown in Fig. 19. This is termed an exponential curve and fish exhibit exponential growth.

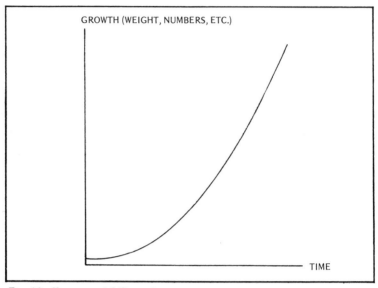

GROWTH (WEIGHT, NUMBERS, ETC.)

TIME

Fig. 19 **Exponential Growth**

A fish gains weight by compound interest and we can work out its daily increase in weight in the same way as we would work out compound interest. If W_0 = the initial weight of the fish and r = the percentage increase in weight per day, then the increase in weight after one day will be:

$$W_0 \times \frac{r}{100}$$

and the total weight at the end of the first day will be:

$$W_0 + \frac{W_0 r}{100} = W_0 \left(1 + \frac{r}{100}\right)$$

The total weight after n days will thus be:

$$W_0 \left(1 + \frac{r}{100}\right)^n$$

In the smallest pond, we have 300 fish with an initial weight of 4.5g each. Our growth target is 30g per fish after six months (182 days), so they will need to increase their weight by:

$$100 \left(\sqrt[182]{\frac{30}{4.5}} - 1 \right) \text{ \% per day}$$

This equation is not really as daunting as it appears. We can easily find the root of a number by looking up the log of the number, dividing it by the root, and then looking up the antilog. If we divide the final weight (30g) by the initial weight (4.5g) and look up the natural log of this answer, we get a figure of 1.8971. If we then divide this by 182 (the root), we arrive at a figure of 0.0104. The antilog of this is 1.0105, and we then subtract 1, to give us 0.0105, and multiply by 100, to give us 1.05. To meet the growth target, the fish therefore need to increase their weight by 1.05% of their body weight per day. Because the food conversion coefficient is 2, we would have to feed them at twice this amount per day to get them to grow at the desired rate, meaning we must distribute 2.1% of their body weight per day.

Table 1. Daily and Weekly Feeding Rates for Pond 1 without Correction for Natural Productivity

Week No.	Predicted Weekly Wt. of Fish (g)	Daily Ration (g) (300 fish)	Weekly Ration (g) (300 fish)
1	4.8	28	198
2	5.2	30	213
3	5.6	32	229
4	6.0	35	246
5	6.5	37	265
6	6.9	40	285
7	7.4	43	307
8	8.0	47	329
9	8.6	50	354
10	9.3	54	381
11	10.0	58	410
12	10.7	63	441
13	11.6	67	475
14	12.4	72	511
15	13.4	78	549
16	14.4	84	591
17	15.5	90	635
18	16.7	97	683
19	17.9	105	735
20	19.3	112	791
21	20.8	121	850
22	22.3	130	915
23	24.0	140	984
24	25.8	151	1059
25	27.8	162	1139
26	29.9	174	1225

14.80kg

In practice, we calculate the weekly ration and feed them the same amount of food per day for seven days at a time, rather than altering the quantity fractionally every day. The calculation of the weekly ration is also based on the actual weight of the fish every week, rather than the theoretical weight, since their growth will fluctuate slightly with variations in prevailing temperature, season etc. Perhaps during one week, there may be a cloud of insects around the pond and the fish will derive some nourishment from this. The theoretical weight provides a check as to how well they are doing each week.

Table 1 shows the increase in weight expected each week if they gain 1.05% of their body weight per day for six months (26 weeks). It also shows the amount to feed each day to 300 fish for 26 weeks, and

Table 2. Daily and Weekly Feeding Rates for Pond 2, Without Correction for Natural Productivity

Week No.	Desired Weekly Wt. of Fish (g)	Daily Ration (g) (300 Fish)	Weekly Ration (g) (300 Fish)
1	30.9	83	587
2	32.0	86	607
3	33.0	89	627
4	34.1	92	647
5	35.3	95	669
6	36.4	98	691
7	37.6	101	714
8	38.9	105	737
9	40.2	108	762
10	41.5	112	787
11	42.9	116	813
12	44.3	119	840
13	45.7	123	868
14	47.3	128	896
15	48.8	132	926
16	50.4	136	957
17	52.1	141	988
18	53.8	145	1021
19	55.7	150	1055
20	57.5	155	1090
21	59.4	160	1126
22	61.3	166	1163
23	63.4	171	1201
24	65.5	177	1241
25	67.6	183	1282
26	69.9	189	1325

23.62kg

the total amount to feed each week. The supplementary food for the first pond should ideally be given in four roughly equal lots throughout the day. This will ensure that all the food is eaten and that digestion is as efficient as possible. It will be remembered that overfeeding of carp may cause some of the food to be voided before it is completely digested. This does not occur to the same extent in trout, but they may not utilise what they eat as completely as is desirable to maintain a satisfactory food conversion.

Pond 2 We can calculate the amount of supplemental food required for the second pond in the same way and table 2 shows the results of these calculations. Here our growth target is 70g in six months, from an initial weight of 30g and the daily food ration as a percentage of body weight is greatly reduced (to 0.932% per day). This is to compensate for the lower average temperatures during the winter months when metabolism, and consequently growth, will be slowed. With normal winter temperatures, the fish should have little difficulty consuming this reduced amount of food, but if the temperature of the ponds falls to 5°C or below at any time, they will cease to grow and feed, so no food should be distributed until after the cold spell.

In the second pond, it will be sufficient to feed the fish three times a day. This is also suitable for the third pond, since they will be fed at less than 2 per cent of their body weight per day as well.

Pond 3 Tables 3 and 4 show the daily and weekly feeding rates for pond 3 for nine months and for the holding facility for six months, making allowances for the weekly removal of four fish after that period. These allowances have been made by calculating:
1) that the fish need to be fed 1.4% of their body weight per day over this period to grow from 70 to 250g.
2) the amount of food required until the fish reach an edible size (after 105 days).
3) The amount of food required by one fish for one week and then multiplying that amount by the number of fish remaining (reduced by four each week).

After the six month's growth to the target weight of 250g has been completed, we have suggested that the daily ration be decreased by 50%, in order that the overall weight of supplementary food used throughout the year is kept to a minimum. This means that the edible fish at the end of the year will weigh about 600g in theory, although in practice they may weigh less than this. If it is desired to produce larger fish, say 1kg each, then feeding could continue at the same percentage of the body weight as before. As we have described it, the farmer would also be left with a hundred extra fish at the end of the year; this would of course not be so in reality. There is always bound to be some mortality throughout the eighteen months, and it is extremely unlikely that exactly 100 fish will be lost in this time. Nor will four fish be removed

Table 3. Daily and Weekly Feeding Rates for Pond 3, Without Correction for Natural Productivity

Week No.	Desired Weekly Wt. of Fish (g)	No. of Fish	Daily Ration (g)	Weekly Ration (g)
1	73	300	294	2061
2	77	300	309	2164
3	81	300	324	2387
4	85	300	340	2273
5	89	300	358	2506
6	93	300	375	2632
7	98	300	394	2765
8	103	300	414	2902
9	108	300	435	3048
10	114	300	457	3200
11	119	300	480	3361
12	125	300	504	3529
13	132	300	529	3706
14	138	300	555	3892
15	145	300	583	4087
16	153	296	604	4234
17	160	292	626	4387
18	168	288	649	4543
19	177	284	672	4704
20	186	280	695	4871
21	195	276	720	5042
22	205	272	745	5218
23	215	268	771	5399
24	226	264	797	5584
25	237	260	835	5776
26	249	256	853	5972
27	256	252	440	3086
28	262	248	445	3118
29	269	244	449	3143
30	275	240	452	3168
31	282	236	456	3192
32	289	232	459	3216
33	296	228	462	3239
34	304	224	465	3261
35	311	220	468	3282
36	319	216	471	3302
37	327	212	474	3321
38	335	208	477	3339
39	343	204	479	3356

142.3kg

Table 4. Daily and Weekly Feeding Rates for the Holding Pond or Tank

Week No.	Weekly Wt of Fish (g)	Fish Remaining	Daily Ration (g)	Weekly Ration (g)
1	352	200	481	3372
2	360	196	483	3386
3	369	192	485	3399
4	378	188	487	3411
5	388	184	488	3421
6	397	180	489	3429
7	407	176	490	3436
8	417	172	491	3441
9	428	168	492	3444
10	438	164	492	3446
11	449	160	492	3445
12	460	156	491	3442
13	472	152	490	3437
14	483	148	489	3429
15	495	144	488	3419
16	508	140	486	3406
17	520	136	484	3391
18	533	132	481	3373
19	546	128	478	3351
20	560	124	475	3327
21	574	120	471	3300
22	588	116	466	3269
23	603	112	461	3234
24	617	108	456	3196
25	633	104	450	3153
26	648	100	443	3107

87.5kg

each week. It is envisaged that fish will be removed as and when they are needed, and this may be ten one week, and none for the following fortnight. How trout are culled is up to the farmer, but the supplementary ration should always be altered accordingly.

It should be emphasised at this point that the feeding schedules shown in Tables 1—4 are theoretical. Although, on average, the trout will increase their weight according to our calculations, the weight of supplementary food shown will vary considerably from week to week when calculated according to the real weight of real fish.

In addition, no correction factor has been incorporated to allow for the maintenance ration that fish require to replace tissues etc., and this becomes increasingly important as the fish get larger. In larger fish, it may be as high as 0.25% of the body weight per day. Although we will discuss maintenance rations in a little more detail in the chapter on nutrition, it is pertinent to state here that maintenance rations are usually expressed as a function of the total energy in the diet.

The total amount of food required for one year's operation of the trout farm is the sum of all the food used in each pond and the holding pond or tank, from March of one year to March of the next. This is about 280kg without any contribution from natural productivity.

Management of the Ponds

There is a good deal more to looking after the fish ponds than throwing in a handful of food three times a day and leaving the fish to get on with it. Once the ponds are under water and stocked with fish, however, daily and weekly management procedures are not really an irksome task.

Management of the ponds can be divided into two sections, the first concerning the preparation and initial stocking of the ponds, and the second the day to day running.

Preparation

When the ponds have been newly constructed one of the first tasks is to test their watertightness and to estimate the losses that may be expected from evaporation and seepage. Seepage may be assessed as the pond is filled. The approximate volume of the pond can be gauged from the dimensions, and the time taken to fill with a constant and known inflow will allow calculation of seepage. A more accurate determination of the total evaporation and seepage losses can be made when the pond is full. The difference between outflow and inflow will indicate total water loss in the pond.

Evaporation will vary with the weather. Warm, dry weather, in conjunction with a prevailing wind, will cause the highest evaporation losses. Conversely, cold and damp winter weather will be associated with the lowest losses.

Seepage will be highest during the first weeks of flooding, as the dyke compacts, settles and becomes saturated with moisture. Thereafter, losses should stabilise.

Total water losses in excess of 2 litres per minute per are usually indicate either a break in the dyke, or insufficient compaction of the dyke material. It has already been mentioned that too many stones or other coarse materials will promote seepage through the dyke and may eventually cause its collapse. We must stress again that the greatest care should be taken in the construction of the dyke and the preparation of the pond bottom, to ensure sufficient compaction of the soil. It is virtually impossible to repair numerous leaks, although some success has been had with hydrated aluminium silicates which swell strongly in water and plug up any small holes. After the initial settling down period, the amount of water required to maintain a constant level in the back-yard ponds should not be more than 0.5–1 litre per minute during normal weather conditions, and never more than 2 litres per minute. If it is greater than this, then methods of sealing the ponds, such as lining with clay, should be considered.

Liming and application of mineral fertilisers should take place before the ponds are put under water although fertilisation will not be necessary for any of the ponds during the first year unless the soil is known to be extremely poor in mineral elements. All improvement procedures should be carried out after the ponds have supported their first fish populations and should be repeated each year when the ponds are drained.

Draining and drying the ponds for a period of time each year has several beneficial effects, the most important of which is the destruction of the encysted stage or of intermediate hosts of organisms which cause fish diseases. Hygienic conditions are especially desirable on a trout farm, as they tend to be more susceptible to diseases than warm water fish.

Drying the pond bottom improves the fertility of the mud, by exposing it to sun and frost, whose action aids the production of a fine tilth and recycling of minerals and nutrients. The practice of cultivation of drained ponds is now dying out, as fish culture intensifies, but there are many excellent traditional techniques which can be of value to the farmer. We suggest that the second pond, which is always dry over the

Fig. 20

45

summer months, should be planted with leguminous plants such as peas, beans or lupins. Not only will this provide an extra crop from the pond area (except in the case of lupins), but it will put nitrogen into the soil and increase the natural productivity when the pond is again put under water. When sowing, the soil of the pond bottom should not be turned over, but should be broken up and mixed to a depth of around 10cm. This retains the most productive humus on the surface, benefitting the productivity of the pond when it is flooded again.

The first pond should be kept dry over the winter, and may be turned over, but should not be planted, except perhaps with grass. It is a good idea to spread a mulch of hay over the bottom of this pond a couple of weeks before it is put under water. This will speed the growth of rotifers and crustacea in the pond before it is stocked, and provide initially a rich food supply for the smallest fish.

The third pond is kept dry from mid-December to mid-March, as far as this is possible, and the bottom should be lightly tilled. Apart from liming and fertilisation, nothing else need be done to this pond.

All the ponds should be put under water 3—4 weeks before they are due to be stocked. This allows the fauna of the pond to become established, and the bottom to settle down again after the dry period.

When the ponds are ready for stocking, the fish should be bought and ready for releasing by mid-morning in the case of the first pond. This allows plenty of daylight to observe them and make sure that they settle down without any problems. Fish from a supplier, unless very close at hand, usually come in a plastic bag pumped up with air or oxygen. They should not be removed from this until temperatures in the pond and the bag are within $2^{o}C$ of one another. If the fish are showing signs of stress, it is a good idea to release them into a large plastic dustbin floated in the pond, until the temperatures are equilibrated. A few fish only should be released to begin with, and these should be observed for a quarter of an hour or so, to make sure that they are quite happy. The rest may then be freed, but they should be checked periodically throughout the course of the day.

If any of the released fish show signs of distress in the pond, the remaining fish should be kept in a dustbin and aerated until the cause of the problem is ascertained. A small aquarium air pump is a very useful acquisition for this purpose. A procedure for problem solving is outlined in the chapter on diseases.

Day to Day Running

The weighing and distribution of the daily food ration is the biggest task of every day. In addition to this a regular check must be made on the inflow and outflow to each pond, especially the screens at these points. The finer the screens, the more liable they will be to clogging, so the first and second ponds will be most at risk. Autumn should be the time for greatest vigilance in this respect, with its abundance of dead leaves, but high winds often cause considerable debris to collect in the ponds. Checking the screens will become a matter of habit each time the fish are fed and will only take a few minutes each day. The volume of the inflow should also be checked frequently, to make sure that it does not vary appreciably, and it should also be increased during hot weather even if the fish are not showing any visible signs of stress. Oxygen levels in the water can fall dramatically after feeding, especially if the fish are not feeding very well (perhaps because of cold) and all the food is not consumed. Never hurry the feeding of the fish — not only can it waste expensive food, but unusual feeding responses are often the first sign of trouble, and should not be overlooked. On the other hand, do not become alarmed by slight sluggishness in response.

Fig. 21

It is worthwhile taking precautions against predators. The worst offenders are herons and kingfishers, although these are no longer so abundant, but the domestic cat is quite adept at taking fish in shallow water. Netting pegged over the ponds is quite effective for keeping out birds. Trout are rather stupid where birds are concerned for they tend to be inquisitive and swim to the surface to take a look, making themselves easy prey. Mink and otters are another potential nuisance in certain areas of Britain. Farmers and countrymen are usually aware of the likely predators in an area, and it does no harm to ask advice from neighbours.

Tank Farming of Rainbow Trout

High density rearing of rainbow trout, relying entirely on the use of artificial diets, is best carried out in circular tanks. Such intensive culture has several useful attributes, namely:

(1) Ease of construction and maintenance of the tanks.

(2) Maximum use of available space.

(3) Hygienic conditions of rearing.

(4) Excellent control over the fish's environment, with close observation of the fish themselves.

The water requirements of the tanks are high, of the same order as the water supply to the ponds. The amount of plumbing needed will again depend on the head of water available, for it is useful to have some back-pressure to facilitate automatic cleaning of the tanks and

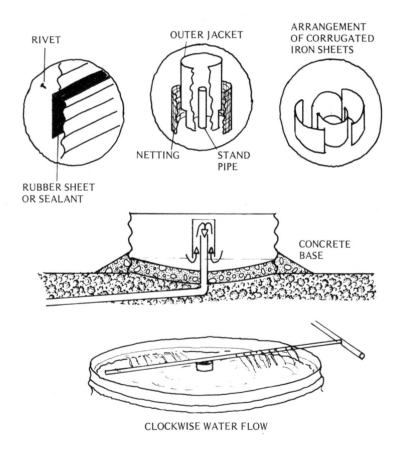

Fig. 22 Corrugated Iron Tanks

allow pre-treatment, such as increased oxygenation, should this be desirable. Total reliance on distributed food will increase costs slightly, but this can be offset by improved food conversion efficiency and faster growth.

Many types of tanks are suitable, made of glass fibre, plastic, brick, concrete or galvanised iron; these can be set into the ground or placed on the surface, whichever is most suitable for supply and drainage purposes. We recommend the use of corrugated galvanised iron tanks, because these are inexpensive and easy to construct, although possessed of poorer durability than fibreglass or plastic. The drawings in fig. 22 show how to construct this type of tank.

Circular tanks are preferred for the even water flow generated in them, which both distributes the fish throughout the whole tank volume and abolishes slack water, making self-cleaning possible. The central drainage pipe with its outer jacket maintains the water level and evacuates excess from the bottom of the tank. This creates an updraught with the outflow, which carries with it all the solids settling out in the centre. The sloping bottom also helps carry the solids towards the centre of the tank, where the slackest water occurs.

The size of the tanks is governed to a certain extent by the commonly available sizes of corrugated iron sheeting, usually 180 x 60cm and 240 x 60cm. Other sizes can be obtained, but at a considerably increased cost. Because there is no contribution from natural productivity, there is no need for fallow periods in the tanks, and they can be used continually throughout the year. High stocking density also reduces the volume requirement considerably, so only two large tanks and one small holding tank are needed. Since the latter is only used to hold fish for three months out of every twelve, this can be dispensed with if all the fish are culled and frozen.

Apart from the limitations imposed by corrugated iron sheet sizes, the volume of the tanks is dictated by the maximum weight of fish held in them at any one time. This maximum weight is reached in each tank only once a year, round about April, which means that for the rest of the year the tanks are understocked. Under-stocking will not hurt the fish, but to economise on space and materials, the tanks should be built with just sufficient capacity to hold their respective maximum weights of fish. If growth is rapid and the tanks become overstocked, then a few extra fish will have to be culled.

We have followed exactly the same stocking schedule as for the trout ponds, with the same growth period (15 months to the first edible fish from initial stocking), but because of the greater control over the fish in tanks, fewer mortalities are likely and only 250 fingerlings need to be bought in each year. This helps to reduce the water requirement because of the reduced total weight of fish. The management and stocking procedure for the two tanks and the holding facility is shown in fig 23, and the feeding and growth rates in tables 5 and 6.

Tank Size

If all the 250 fish in tank one survive to reach their desired individual weight of 70g, then the total weight at the end of this twelve month would be 17.5kg. Stocking densities in intensive culture are usually between 0.016 and 0.096kg per litre, and we would recommend stocking densities between 0.016 and 0.032kg per litre. At the lowest stocking density of 0.016kg per litre, we would need a volume of about 1100 litres to accommodate our 17.5kg of fish at the end of the first year. With the highest stocking densities, the water needs to be maintained at 100% oxygen saturation at all times, and there is a very high risk of large fish losses if oxygen levels should drop. Our recommended stocking densities are quite high, but not too risky in that oxygen levels could fall to 50% of saturation values at temperatures below 15^oC without incurring any mortalities.

If four sheets of 240 x 60cm corrugated iron are used to construct the first tank, this will give a diameter of approximately 1.53 metres, and a volume of 1800 litres if the depth of water is 1 metre. This is more than adequate to contain 250 seventy g fish, and is easy to engineer because the sheets of corrugated iron form a complete semi-circle.

If cropping and growth were to occur exactly as we have predicted, then maximum total weight in the second tank would occur during week 37, when the fish each weigh 327.17g and there are 162 left! This maximum weight would be 53kg, which would need a volume of 3300 litres at our suggested stocking density. If tank 2 is made from six 240 x 60cm sheets of corrugated iron, then the diameter will be 2.28 metres, and the volume about 4000 litres with a water depth of 1 metre. Again this will be more than adequate to contain the expected weight of fish.

Water Requirements

Provided that the water supply is always at or near oxygen saturation, relatively free of suspended solids, and at or below 15^oC, we can work on the basis of a water requirement of 1 litre per minute per 2kg of fish weight. We suggest jetting the water into the tanks (see fig 22) to increase oxygenation. This is one of the simplest and most efficient means of aerating the water, whilst at the same time generating a fast circular flow in the tanks, sweeping faeces and other settled matter to the outflow. Flow should be clockwise in the northern hemisphere, and a series of pipes will have to be made, with progressively larger holes, to accommodate the increased water requirement as the fish grow.

In the first tank, water supply should begin at about 2 litres per minute, and be increased to 9–10 litres per minute over the year as the fish approach 70g each. It should begin at this value in the second tank, and be increased to 23–26 litres per minute by week 25. Should the

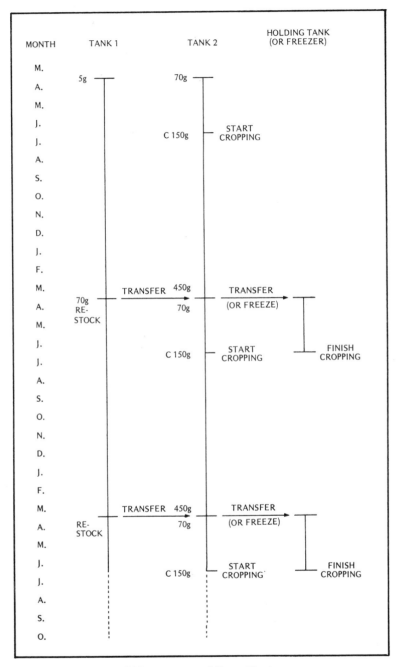

Fig. 23 **Stocking and Management of Trout Tanks**

51

temperature rise above 15°C, however, flow rate may need to be increased if the fish show any signs of stress.

General Husbandry

As with the trout ponds, the tanks can be cropped earlier during the first year if the second tank is stocked with half the usual number of 70g fish at the same time as the first tank. Edible fish will then be available from the third month after stocking, but the initial cost of these will of course be higher than the cost of 30g fish bought in for the ponds.

Maintenance of the tanks is less complicated than the ponds, because there are no fallow periods and no need for fertilisation. Food should be distributed three or four times a day, depending on the size of the fish, and the only checks necessary are on inflow and outflow to ensure these are clear, and daily temperature to ensure that the fish have enough water to satisfy their respiratory requirements. Recordings of weekly weight of a sample of fish should be kept, to adjust the food ration, and assess the progress of the stock. Although the suggested feeding schedules are based on a food conversion of 2:1 as before, in practice the conversion ratio may be better than this. Knowing the weight of the fish and the amount of food distributed, the food conversion can be estimated and the amount of food altered accordingly. Dissolved oxygen should be determined at least once a fortnight and more frequently during hot weather. Since trout have a tendency to jump, both tanks should be permanently covered with a net or solid lid. A solid lid must not block out the light, for trout are sight feeders and will only take food in the light.

Tanks based on a throughflow of water are the simplest and least time-consuming method of keeping rainbow trout, and once the fish have reached an edible size, they need only be fed every other day if this is preferred, to maintain their weight; but they should always be checked every day, for it is at the time of least attention that problems always (perversely) occur.

Commercial Fish Food

Since we recommend the use of commercial trout pellets as supplemental food in the backyard trout ponds, we must make some mention of them here. There are many suppliers of fish food in Europe and the USA, most of which are subsiduaries of firms mainly concerned with animal feeds.

Between them, the European firms manufacture compounded feeds for predominantly salmon, trout, carp and eels, American companies produce diets for trout, salmon and channel catfish. All products in Europe are marketed at very similar prices, sizes and quality. There is slightly more variation amongst American companies.

Trout feeds are generally marketed as 'crumbles' for the very

Table 5. Feeding Schedules for Tank 1

Week No.	Predicted Weekly Wt of Fish (g)	Daily Ration (g) (250 Fish)	Weekly Ration (g) (250 Fish)
1	4	23	165
2	5	25	177
3	5	27	191
4	6	29	205
5	6	31	221
6	6	33	237
7	7	36	255
8	8	39	274
9	8	42	295
10	9	45	318
11	10	48	341
12	10	52	368
13	11	56	395
14	12	60	425
15	13	65	458
16	14	70	492
17	15	75	530
18	16	81	569
19	17	87	613
20	19	94	659
21	20	101	709
22	22	108	762
23	24	117	820
24	25	126	882
25	27	135	949
26	29	145	1021
			reduced ration
27	30	69	489
28	32	72	505
29	33	74	522
30	34	77	540
31	35	79	557
32	36	82	576
33	37	84	595
34	38	87	615
35	40	90	635
36	41	93	656
37	42	96	678
38	44	99	700
39	45	103	723
40	47	106	747
41	48	110	772
42	50	113	797
43	52	117	824
44	53	121	851
45	55	125	879
46	57	129	908
47	59	134	938
48	61	138	969
49	63	143	1001
50	65	147	1034
51	67	152	1068
52	69	157	1104

32kg

53

Table 6 Feeding Schedule for Tank 2

Week No.	Predicted Weekly Wt of Fish (g)	Daily Ration (g) (250 Fish)	Weekly Ration (g) (250 Fish)
1	73	245	1717
2	77	257	1804
3	81	270	1894
4	85	284	1989
5	89	298	2088
6	93	313	2193
7	98	329	2303
8	103	345	2418
9	108	362	2540
10	114	380	2667
11	119	400	2801
12	125	420	2941
13	132	441	3088
14	138	463	3243
15	145	486	3406
16	153	510	3576
17	160	527	3696
18	168	545	3818
19	177	563	3942
20	186	581	4071
21	195	600	4201
22	205	619	4335
23	215	638	4472
24	226	658	4611
25	237	679	4754
26	249	699	4899
27	256	354	2478
28	262	355	2489
29	269	357	2499
30	275	358	2508
31	282	359	2516
32	289	360	2523
33	296	361	2529
34	304	361	2533
35	311	362	2536
36	319	362	2538
37	327	362	2538
38	335	362	2537
39	343	361	2534
40	352	361	2529
41	360	360	2522
42	369	359	2514
43	378	357	2504
44	388	355	2491
45	397	353	2477
46	407	351	2460
47	417	348	2441
48	428	345	2419
49	438	342	2395
50	449	338	2368
51	460	334	2339
52	472	329	2306

148kg

small fish up to 10cm and pellets for the larger fish. All are nutritionally complete and provide protein, energy and essential vitamins and minerals. They can therefore be used as a sole food source with complete safety.

One of the disadvantages of using commercial diets on the small fish farm, apart from the cost, is the unit packaging system. Cost is to some extent compensated for by convenience, but nearly all the firms supply in minimum quantities of 25kg, except for the finest fry foods. Because of the deterioration of vitamins and fats, these bags should not be kept for longer than three months unless they are refrigerated. Even then, their useful life is only extended to six months. Unless smaller amounts can be purchased by special arrangement, this makes life very difficult.

For the size range of fish kept in the trout ponds throughout the eighteen months, according to most manufacturers' instructions five different sizes of food would be required, each supplied in 25kg minimum quantities. This would mean there would be too much food for the smallest fish. A way round this is to buy larger food than is needed, and by judicious juggling of freezing and breaking down into smaller sizes, feed it to a greater size range of fish than it is intended. This does have its dangers, because feeds for the smaller fish are formulated slightly differently and at least 10% of the food will be wasted as dust. However, provided pellets no larger than 3mm are used in this way, the difference in composition will not be too critical.

Despite the differences in designation, most commercial pellets have approximately the same size differences, as follows:

1.6mm diameter crumb   — for fingerlings between 6—10cm long
1.6—2mm diameter pellet — for fish between 10—15cm long
2.1—3mm diameter pellet — for fish between 15—20cm long
4—5mm diameter pellet   — for fish between 20—28cm long
6—7mm diameter pellet   — for fish over 28cm long

For the first pond over its six month's use, a total of 14.8kg of supplemental food is required. In this time the fish grow from an initial weight of 4.5g (6—8cm length) to 30g (12—15cm length), so they would ideally need to progress from a 1.5mm diameter crumb to a 2mm diameter pellet in this time. At the same time the third pond will require 100.23kg of supplemental food, consisting of approximately 20kg of 2.1—3mm diameter pellets, 60kg of 4—5mm pellets and 20kg of 6—7mm pellets. During the first half of the six months, the holding tank requires about 6kg of the largest pellets (if these fish are not culled).

The total weight of food required during the first six months of a year's operation is therefore about 120kg, including all the sizes of pellets. If five bags of food were bought, consisting of one bag of 2.1—3mm pellets, three bags of 4—5mm pellets, and one bag of 6—7mm pellets, then all the fish could be fed with food of roughly the right size for their age. The smallest pellets would have to be broken down and frozen for the smallest fish of pond one into the first two size ranges. In addition, three steel or brass mesh sieves are required of 2, 1.5 and 1mm aperture, in order to make fingerling crumbles from the larger pellets.

During the second six months of a year's operation, the second pond requires a total of 23.62kg of food and the fish grow from 30g (12—15cm length) to 70g (18—20cm length), and should progress from a 2mm pellet to a 3mm pellet. During the three months corresponding to the first three months of the second pond's use, the third pond requires 42kg of the largest (6—7mm diameter) pellets and during the last three months of the year the holding tank will require about 6.5kg of the same size pellets. One bag of 2.1—3mm pellets and two bags of the largest pellets would therefore suffice. The bag of 2.1—3mm pellets need only be slightly broken down, and this is best accomplished by hand as they are being fed to the fish. This will reduce the amount lost to powder considerably.

It is recommended that only a month's supply of food be removed from cold storage at any one time, as this will ensure that the food remains in a good condition with minimum degradation of the sensitive vitamins and fats.

4 pond culture of mirror carp

Carp are traditionally a pond fish in Europe, so there is a good deal of information on their extensive and semi-intensive culture. However, intensive culture methods similar to those developed for rainbow trout are only employed where suitable thermal effluents or hot springs can provide the constant high temperatures necessary for optimal growth. Outdoor farming is therefore limited by climate, but indoor rearing of fry in artificially heated water is quite often practised because of the very high value of the product.

Much of what has already been said about the construction and running of trout ponds applies to all fish, and we need not repeat our previous discussions. What we will do is point out the differences.

The Growth Target

Under ideal conditions carp can grow from egg to 2kg adult in one year. Since they are a warm water species 'ideal conditions' means a constant temperature of about 28°C, good quality water and an abundance of food. Carp in ponds with seasonal changes in temperature and little supplementary feeding usually require three years to achieve this weight in temperate climates, but this is still fast growth when it is considered that significant weight increase only occurs for four or five months of summer each year. This is the reason for the common division of carp into three age/weight classes, referred to as one, two and three summer old fish. One summer mirror carp most often weigh about 50g and measure 9–12cm, two summer carp about 300–400g (22–25cm) and three summer carp about 1.5kg (40–45cm).

We suggest they are culled for eating when they reach about 400–500g, which is twice the weight of table sized rainbow trout. Fish of this size are readily prepared for cooking because the fine intermuscular bones and external scales can be removed more easily.

Carp flesh is also reputed to improve in flavour and texture with age, so this size strikes a balance between optimum pond use and gastronomic acceptability.

It should be possible to produce 500g mirror carp in fifteen months, starting from 5g fingerlings, provided that reasonable summer temperatures are encountered.

Construction of the Ponds

There should be three ponds, each around one are in size, plus a small holding pond or tank. The increase in area is for 3 main reasons: firstly, the overall weight of fish for a year's supply is effectively doubled to 100kg, because of the greater table weight. Secondly, larger ponds require less inflow which will help keep temperatures high throughout the summer and thirdly, because carp are omnivorous and utilise natural food more completely than trout, larger ponds mean more natural food and less supplementary feeding.

The three ponds should be built side by side and supplied with water in a parallel fashion — this will minimise disease hazards. Because carp are so uncompetitive and docile, it is still common practice to keep all sizes together in one pond and crop the larger individuals, but a serious disease outbreak would then mean complete loss of the fish. Keeping the age groups separate in three ponds facilitates harvesting and grading as well.

All the ponds should be made by erecting an earth embankment with an integral monk. If it is at all possible to engineer, the ponds should be drainable because carp are one of the most difficult fish to catch. If the ponds cannot be made drainable, then they should be half the depth we suggest and wintering facilities will have to be provided separately. Unlike the trout ponds, the carp ponds should be dried out for at least three months every year and this should be allowed for when moving the fish.

Shape and Depth

The shape of the ponds is immaterial as long as they can be drained and are of a suitable depth, but it will be remembered that square ponds require the shortest lengths of dyke. Three square ponds side by side with parallel water supply and drainage would be perfectly adequate.

The first pond which is used for holding the smallest carp should be about 1.2 to 1.5 metres deep. The monk is used to regulate the water depth throughout the year, and it should begin at about 2/3 rds of a metre when the pond is stocked at the start of the growing season, and increased to its full depth in September—October, or as soon as the water temperature drops significantly. This will promote rapid warming during the summer and prolong the growing season of the carp. If possible, all the ponds should be in a sunny, south facing position and sheltered by some form of windbreak such as a hedge or brushwood screen, but this must not overshadow the ponds.

The second pond need not be so deep as the first because it is only under water for the warmest months of the year, and a depth of 1 metre will be adequate. This pond should be stocked with fish removed from the first pond in mid-February, or later if water temperatures have not reached 10°C. Small carp should not be moved after a prolonged cold spell until they have recommenced active feeding, which usually occurs when water temperatures reach 10–15°C, because this stresses them and may be a cause of mortality.

The third pond really functions as a holding and overwintering facility for the table sized fish, rather than a growing pond, and for this reason should be quite deep, between 1.5 and 1.75 metres. The carp are held in this pond from September until the following April or May, and will gain little weight in this time. They will also need only a minimal amount of supplementary food. The increased depth will safeguard the fish against a winter freeze, but will make catching fish for eating more difficult. However, cold water makes carp sluggish and they can be quite easily netted after a little practice. Do this with care to avoid disturbing the fish and the pond bottom. The last few carp will have to be caught by draining the pond and transferring them to a holding tank, or freezer.

Stocking the Ponds

The stocking and management strategy for the carp ponds is basically the same as that for the trout. Apart from being friendly, easy to keep and excellent to eat, mirror carp are also very hardy. In Europe, their slightly higher cost in comparison with trout can be offset by the initial purchase of fewer fish, because we can expect lower mortality. Losses of approximately 15% are allowed for throughout the rearing process, and the first pond should accordingly be stocked with 250 fingerling mirror carp each weighing about 5g, and measuring 7cm. The yield in numbers after fifteen months growth will be about the same as the trout ponds, but will be twice the weight, making the carp ponds much more productive. Fingerling mirror carp are usually available from September to April in Europe, but should not be bought for stocking the first pond until average water temperatures have reached 10°C.

The fish in the first pond may be expected to grow from 5 to 100g during the first summer, and they will derive a substantial part of their food from the pond. After wintering, these carp can be transferred to the second pond in February to March (depending on the water temperature), and may be expected to reach an edible size of 500g over the next 5–6 months. There will always be a few fish that will grow considerably faster than the others, called 'jumpers' or 'shooters', and these must be removed as soon as they are large enough to eat. Removal

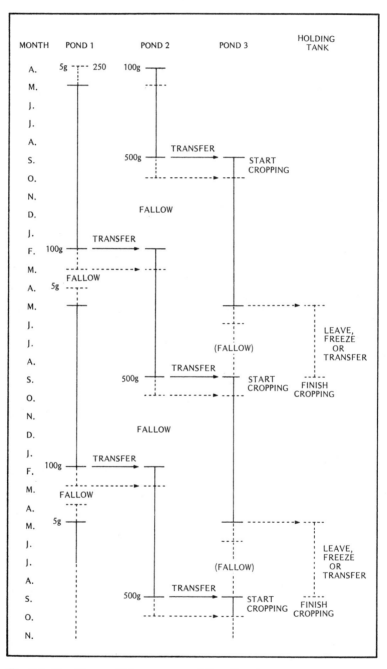

Fig. 24 **Stocking and Management of Carp Ponds**

of such fish will lead after a few weeks to another group of 'shooters' appearing, and these must be selectively cropped in the same way.

The second pond will require the largest proportion of the supplementary food. During the first year, to speed up the production of table sized fish, the second pond can be stocked with 100g fish at the same time as the first pond is stocked with fingerlings, and cropping can then commence after 5 months.

Water Requirements

To maintain a high temperature in the growing ponds throughout the summer months, water inflow should be as small as possible. For the fastest growth, water temperatures should stay between 15 and 28°C, the latter being the optimum for growth and the former the minimum. Below 15°C, food intake is greatly reduced, and at or below 5°C feeding ceases altogether. In all ponds, the water flow should be adjusted to keep the fish happy, and not kept at a pre-determined rate.

Water inflow in the first pond should just compensate for losses due to evaporation and seepage, for there should be no need to supply respiratory water to such a small weight of fish. In special circumstances, the water supply may need to be increased. The culturist should always keep a weather eye open for the first signs of breathing stress, usually air gulping at the surface.

There should always be some surplus water in the second pond because of the greater weight of fish, and it should begin at about 2—3 litres per minute and be increased over the summer to around 8 litres per minute.

During winter, if the surface of either the first or the third pond becomes frozen over, some water flow should be maintained under the ice. This should be just enough to ensure a complete change of water in the ponds about once a week, and not so fast as to cause the fish to swim actively. Skating on or breaking the ice must be avoided, for the fish should be undisturbed.

Where inflows are greater than losses due to evaporation and seepage, screens must be placed at the outflow to prevent escapes. A 1cm aperture screen would suffice for the first pond, and 3 and 5cm aperture screens for the second and third ponds respectively. These should be cared for in exactly the same way as we have already described for screens in the trout ponds.

Natural Productivity

The food produced naturally in a pond plays a much more important part in carp culture than in trout farming. Cyprinids are efficient exploiters of natural productivity because their less discriminatory feeding utilises a greater proportion of the natural food chains. Mirror carp will feed on plankton, crustacea, insects and their larvae, aquatic vegetation and general detritus, and will help to improve natural productivity by their burrowing and rooting around on the pond bottom, so hastening the recycling of nutrients. Carp will also accept a wide range of supplemental foods, of both animal and plant origin. Keeping carp is somewhat like keeping the aquatic equivalent of pigs!

To make the most of natural productivity, fertilisation of the ponds is essential, but the actual effect this will have on the growth of the carp is impossible to predict. It is really a case of 'try it and see', for every pond will have a different response to fertilisation. In the trout ponds, natural food contributes little to growth, so it is relatively easy to calculate the amount of supplementary food required to meet the growth targets we have set. This is not true for the carp ponds, and the first year of operation will have to be spent in determining the natural productivity in order to maximise growth in the following years.

Fertilisation with Inorganic Fertilisers

We have already discussed the action of fertilisers in the pond, and the role of liming as both a pre-conditioner and disinfectant. It is very important to provide initially a neutral or slightly alkaline pond bottom, which will enhance the beneficial effects of fertilisation and improve the water quality. Inorganic fertilisers providing Phosphorous, Potassium and Nitrogen usually exert the greatest effect on pond fertility, and Phosphorous especially is most often found in limiting quantities.

Phosphate Fertilisers In almost all studies, phosphate fertilisers have increased the total yield to some extent, and most waters would appear to be deficient in phosphate. Mineral phosphate fertiliser is available in several forms, of which the most common are superphosphate and basic slag, and they vary in solubility and phosphorous content. Basic slag contains other elements such as calcium and magnesium, and is relatively insoluble, so it is most suited to waters of low pH and poor buffering capacity which are associated with pond bottoms unable to bind minerals. Alkaline soils benefit more from superphosphate applications, because they can hold and gradually release this more soluble form.

The amount of phosphate fertiliser required will depend upon the pond, but will be somewhere in the region of 1 to 3kg per are.

Successful fertilisation is frequently denoted by the production of an algal bloom during the summer, which will tinge the water green. The natural food as a result of fertilisation may be expected to increase by 50 to 200% in favourable circumstances.

Nitrogen Fertilisers. The case for nitrogen fertilisers is not so well established; lack of phosphorous has been shown to inhibit the uptake of nitrogen by flora from the pond, and the ratio of phosphorous to nitrogen is therefore more important. The common sources, sodium nitrate and ammonium fertilisers, are equally effective and should be applied to new ponds that have not had chance to develop a rich mud. Thereafter, nitrogen should not be a limiting factor if the ponds are regularly cultivated with nitrogen fixing plants, but it is worthwhile testing the effect of nitrogen fertilisers on established ponds to determine whether they have a beneficial action. Nitrogen fertilisers are normally applied at about 0.5 to 1 kg per are.

Potassium Fertilisers. Potassium is like nitrogen in that it is likely to be of use in poorer ponds only. It does promote the growth of submerged vegetation, and is available as kainit, which contains potassium chloride and magnesium sulphate, and this should be distributed at 1—2 kg per are.

Before the ponds are put under water for the first time, we suggest fertilising each with 1—2 kg of a 1:1:1 mixture of an NPK fertiliser, usually available from seed merchants or agricultural suppliers. The ponds are then gradually filled, and the initial algal bloom which should cause a thick green scum to form on the water will fade after 7—10 days and be replaced by a grey-blue to brown colouration, which signifies the development of microfauna feeding off the algae. Stocking should begin at this point. The application may be repeated in the first pond after two months, or when the blue-grey or brown colouration fades. In trout ponds, although the same application rates are generally suitable, the ponds must not be put under water until a week to ten days after fertilisation, otherwise the through flow will rapidly leach out the fertilisers before they become absorbed into the pond bottom.

Fertilisation with Organic Fertilisers

Manure has been used for a long time to increase the fertility of carp ponds, and is very effective because it contains all the elements essential for floral and faunal growth, together with an ability to form a rich productive mud. It also carries one great danger; over-generous application rapidly depletes dissolved oxygen and results in mass mortality. Distributed carefully and in small quantities at any one time, there is no better growth promoter for carp ponds.

The best organic fertilisers are those in an advanced state of decomposition. 'Ripe' manures, liquid or solid, can contain a great deal of ammonia, which is poisonous to the fish. Animal manures are preferably applied in bulk before the ponds are flooded, and should be placed in discreet heaps on the pond bottom at about 20—40kg to the are. Green manures can be provided by cut plants, either those grown in the ponds during the dry period or crop plants, but both should be used before the ponds are put under water, and not after.

Regular distribution of animal manure throughout the summer can be beneficial, but should not exceed 10kg every three weeks. The major disadvantage of repeated manuring is silting up of the ponds, and dredging may be necessary every other year during the dry period to maintain their depth. Organic manuring should be in addition to, not instead of inorganic fertilisation. The mud produced by the organic manure aids the activity of the inorganic fertiliser.

Keeping ducks on carp ponds is one well-established way of

increasing natural productivity, for the duck droppings act as an excellent fertiliser while the birds themselves represent a valuable secondary crop. If ducks are kept on the carp ponds, organic manure should be restricted to the dry periods to avoid over-fertilisation, and may not be necessary at all if the ponds are naturally productive.

Heavy white breeds of duck have been found to be best, but it would be better to choose ducks for their laying capacity rather than their meat, because no more than 3 or 4 should be kept on each pond. One of the best layers available in Britain is known as the Khaki Campbell breed. Ducks may derive as much as 30% of their food from the pond, and it should be possible to grow 3kg birds in the same time as it takes to grow the carp to their yearly target weights.

Supplementary Feeding

Supplementary food must be distributed in the first and second ponds to ensure the carp meet the growth targets, and in the third pond to keep them healthy over the winter, but the amount will vary according to the amount of natural food in the pond. Instead of a weekly feeding schedule, we have listed the weekly growth increments required

Table 7 Desired Weekly Weight Increases for Carp Pond 1

Week No.	Weekly Weight (5 months) g	Weekly Weight (4 months) g
1	5.7	5.9
2	6.6	7.1
3	7.6	8.4
4	8.7	9.9
5	10.0	11.8
6	11.4	14.0
7	13.1	16.7
8	15.1	19.8
9	17.3	23.5
10	19.9	27.9
11	22.8	33.1
12	26.2	39.3
13	30.0	46.7
14	34.5	55.4
15	39.6	65.8
16	45.4	78.2
17	52.1	92.8
18	59.9	99.9
19	68.7	
20	78.9	
21	90.6	
22	99.9	

Table 8 Desired Weekly Weight Increases for Carp Pond 2

Week No.	Weekly Weight (5 months) g	Weekly Weight (4 months) g
1	107.7	109.7
2	116.0	120.3
3	124.9	131.9
4	134.5	144.7
5	144.8	158.6
6	156.0	174.0
7	168.0	190.8
8	180.9	209.2
9	194.8	229.5
10	209.8	251.6
11	225.9	276.0
12	243.3	302.6
13	262.0	331.9
14	282.1	364.0
15	303.8	399.2
16	327.2	437.7
17	352.4	480.1
18	379.5	499.4
19	408.6	
20	440.1	
21	473.9	
22	499.6	

to meet the growth targets for ponds 1 and 2. Tables 7 and 8 show these expected weekly weights for growing seasons of four and five months, since a late winter may delay stocking.

The best way to calculate the supplementary food required is to sample the ponds at weekly intervals, and compare the average weight of the fish with the desired weekly weight shown in the tables. If stocking begins in May, then the five month tables should be consulted, but if not until June, then the same growth will have to be made in four months.

The culturist should aim to reach the four and five months growth target in each pond by the end of September, when temperatures are likely to fall sharply. If the youngest carp do not reach 100g during their first summer, this can fairly easily be made up by extra feeding during the second summer, and should not be a cause for concern.

To reach 100g in 22 weeks, the carp in the first pond would have to increase their body weight by almost 2% per day, while in 18 weeks, a 2.5% per day increase would be required. If the water is warm enough, carp are quite capable of growing at 4% of their body weight per day, so these rates are readily attainable. In the second pond, growth does not need to be quite so rapid, 5 and 4 month growing periods requiring 1.06 and 1.33% daily increases respectively. These leave scope for making up growth deficiencies from the first year.

The Type of Supplementary Food The natural food of carp in ponds is reckoned to be rich in protein (up to 60% of the diet), and it is common practice in semi-intensive methods of carp farming to distribute supplementary food composed mainly of carbohydrates. By supplying energy, these carbohydrate − rich foods 'spare' some of the natural protein by allowing it to be turned into fish protein instead of energy. Supplemental foods of this type commonly consist of cereals like rye, wheat, barley and maize, or pulses such as lupin, pea or soya. The pulses are quite high in protein and make good supplemental food for carp.

It is better to feed with a variety of supplemental feeds of this kind rather than just one, because a mixture is more likely to satisfy the nutritional requirements of the carp. We also suggest combining the traditional fattening foods with a small amount of commercial trout or carp diet, to ensure the fish get an adequate supply of essential amino acids and vitamins. Some carp farmers use commercial pelleted diets for chickens and pigs as supplemental food, with good results, for these are fairly high in carbohydrate but contain vitamin and mineral mixes not very different from those incorporated in fish diets.

Carp will accept all sorts of feedstuffs, and the backyard farmer should experiment for himself with whatever he has available. Numerous articles have reported that carp can be fed on kitchen scraps, but this is not strictly true. If the fish can be seen to accept vegetable peelings, it will do no harm to distribute a few, but on no account should these form a large part of the diet. A wide variety of reasonable quality food will ensure the carp meet the growth targets, and this should always be borne in mind.

Extending the Growing Season

Because the growth of carp in ponds is so dependent on temperature, prolonging the growing season in temperate climates means maintaining suitable temperatures for a greater proportion of the year. Fortunately however, the combined use of solar water heaters and cheap polyethylene greenhouses is both a workable and attractive proposition for heating outdoor ponds.

Experiments in Britain and the U.S.A. have demonstrated the feasibility of this idea, and shown that together solar panels and greenhouse insulation will raise temperatures about $10^\circ C$ above those of an open pond. Horticultural greenhouses alone can raise water temperatures by about $5^\circ C$. Stocking of the ponds could begin 1−2 months earlier than normal, and growth could continue for an extra month into Autumn, extending the total growing season to six months.

If the two carp growing ponds were to be covered with polyethy-

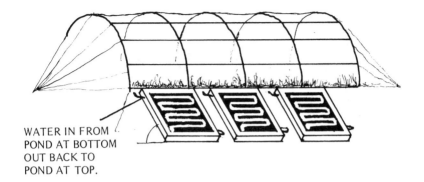

WATER IN FROM
POND AT BOTTOM
OUT BACK TO
POND AT TOP.

Fig. 25 **Pond in Polythene Greenhouse with Solar Panels**

lene greenhouses, they would need to be long and thin (although of the same area) because the commercially available greenhouses are oblong. A five metre wide by twenty metre long pond could be enclosed quite easily and for a reasonable cost. Installing additional solar panels would increase costs considerably, especially if these are bought rather than home-made, but may be worth it in the long term. They do not need to be as efficient as panels for domestic water heating, but they would need a large surface area to increase pond temperatures significantly. The type of collectors used for heating swimming pools are suitable.

5 channel catfish and tilapia

Channel catfish and tilapia are not as suited to pond culture as carp and trout in temperate climates. Channel catfish can only be cultured in the U.S.A. because of import restrictions in Europe, and tilapia are unable to withstand the low temperatures typical of temperate winters. The following account of their small-scale pond culture is therefore necessarily brief.

The Pond Culture of Channel Catfish

The culture requirements of channel catfish are a cross between those of trout and carp, in that they are a warm-water species, but intolerant of poor oxygen conditions. Best growth occurs when temperatures range from 22 to 30°C, although the fish will feed and grow slowly even at 10°C. The constraints imposed by dissolved oxygen mean that ponds have to be larger and stocking density lower than that employed in carp culture, although general husbandry techniques are very similar.

The accepted table weight for channel catfish is usually quoted as being 450g, so the total weight of fish required will be about 90kg over the year. It should be possible to produce 450g channel catfish in fifteen months, starting from 5—10cm fingerlings, much the same growth rate as carp and occurring during the same months.

There should be three growing ponds, one of 1 are for the fingerlings, the other two between 1.5 and 2 ares. Larger ponds are required to meet both the oxygen requirements of the fish and to provide a good quantity of natural food. Channel catfish do not utilise the natural food organisms in a pond as completely as carp, even though they are omnivorous, so it is worthwhile increasing the available food supply by extending the area if possible. Apart from size, all the other instructions for the construction of the carp ponds apply to the catfish ponds, including depth regulation during winter. Although water warming will be facilitated by minimum inflow during the spring and summer, more southerly areas of the U.S.A. experiencing hot summers will need a substantial water inflow to prevent excessive warming.

'Channel catfish' can be substituted for the word 'carp' in most of the previous section on carp farming, the biggest difference between the two species being their tolerance to environmental quality. Channel catfish are indigenous to the great rapid water courses of the Mississipi basin from the region of the great lakes to the Gulf of Mexico and are consequently well-suited to turbid water rich in dissolved oxygen; they are not particularly suited to a still water pond habitat. When water temperatures are high, it is more difficult to maintain adequate levels of dissolved oxygen because of the reducing solubility of oxygen in water. Balancing the amount of water inflow to supply sufficient oxygen while maintaining temperatures in a pond at a level which optimises growth can be a great problem, unless inflow water is also at a high temperature. Surface water is best from this point of view, although at the height of summer when water is needed most, surface water may not supply sufficient flow to cool and re-oxygenate the pond.

Stocking and Growth

In commercial catfish culture in the southern states of the U.S.A., table sized (450g) fish can be produced in 180 days from April to October when the ponds are initially stocked with 15cm (30g) fingerlings. These are intensively fed on artificial diets, with little contribution from natural food. The extended growing season of 6 to 7 months due to the favourable climate greatly aids production of this type. More northerly states experience a growing season comparable to that in Europe, of only 4 to 5 months duration, and based on this channel catfish would require fifteen months to grow from 6–8cm (about 5g) to 450g.

Channel catfish are fairly hardy but more excitable than carp. They need to be disturbed as little as possible during the growing season to prevent wastage of food. Smaller fingerlings than those preferred commercially can be used in the ponds, as this cuts down costs considerably, but does enhance the risk of greater losses. Overall losses throughout the fifteen months should not be greater than 15%, and the first pond should therefore be stocked with 250 6–8cm fish. Their growth target throughout is identical with the growth targets of the carp, and the tables for the desired weight increases of the carp should be consulted. During the first summer, the fingerling channel catfish should be able to reach 150g, but they will not make as great a proportion of this growth on natural food as would carp, and supplementary food should be distributed, as required, to meet the growth target.

After wintering, the channel catfish should be transferred to the second pond in February or March (depending on water temperature, which should have reached 10°C) and may be expected to have reached an edible size by the following August.

The third pond is also used as a holding and overwintering facility for the table sized catfish, and should be of the same depth as the third carp pond. They are kept in this pond from September until the following April or May, and will gain little weight in this time.

Water Supply
Unless temperatures are excessive, the first pond should not require respiratory water until the catfish reach about 80g each, and inflows should just compensate for losses due to evaporation and seepage. Towards the end of June, as the fish are growing rapidly and temperatures are reaching a maximum, water inflow to the first pond should gradually be increased, until at the end of the growing season it is about 5—8 litres per minute. (This is only meant as a guide, water inflows being matched to the needs of the fish.) Because of their susceptibility to oxygen depletion, the fish must be watched for any signs of stress. The earliest warning of something amiss is reduced aggressiveness during feeding and feeding should be stopped altogether for a while to prevent further oxygen depletion.

Respiratory water should be provided at all times in the second pond during the summer, beginning at about 5 litres per minute and increasing to 10—15 litres per minute in the Autumn. Only a small inflow (about 1—2 litres per minute) will be required in the third pond during the winter.

Catfish ponds of the size we recommend should not be constructed if a water supply with a minimum flow of 30 litres per minute is not available. It is desirable always to have an unused potential of 10—15 litres per minute just in case it should ever be needed to replenish the water quickly in any of the ponds. In the absence of such a supply, the size of all the ponds should be doubled for the same stocking density to provide adequate insurance against a fishkill.

Fertilisation
Inorganic fertilisation during the fallow periods is desirable to optimise production of natural food, but organic fertilisers should be avoided. Manures are reputed to taint the flesh of the catfish, but the major reason for avoiding fertilisation while the ponds are under water is to prevent oxygen depletion. At the relatively high stocking density of catfish ponds, the margin between adequate and insufficient oxygenation is very small and addition of organic matter in the quantities suggested for the carp ponds could very easily deplete oxygen to a lethal level.

Inorganic fertilisers should be distributed at the rates previously described for trout and carp ponds, although the results will depend on the individual ponds. Organic manure in half the quantities suggested for the carp ponds may be applied before the ponds are put under water.

Supplementary Feeding

Because channel catfish are very prone to the establishment of feeding hierarchies when the food is of variable composition, it has been found that pelleted supplemental food gives each fish an equal opportunity to feed, thus producing more even growth within a pond population and improved food conversion. A minimum of 32% protein in these rations is required if growth is to be optimised.

Although catfish go into a feeding frenzy rather like rainbow trout when supplementary food is distributed, not all the pellets are eaten at one time. For this reason, it is common practice to place a submerged 'feeding table' in each pond, consisting of a 1—2 metre diameter plate (of a light colour) 50 to 70cm below the water surface. The food is always dispersed above this plate, and uneaten food falls onto its surface. This allows the catfish chance to mop up the uneaten food, and also allows the culturist to gauge the appetite of his fish. If uneaten food remains on the table ten minutes or so after the fish have been fed, then this provides some indication of the well being of the fish. A reduced appetite is the first symptom of a drop in oxygen levels or environmental quality, and is often a sufficiently early warning to allow diagnosis and correction without any loss of fish.

Since feeding always results in depletion of dissolved oxygen to some extent, it is very important not to overfeed the fish, especially when other factors such as high water temperature can aggravate such a mistake. Appetite is naturally reduced at high and low temperatures but the maximum safe feeding rate is approximately 3% of the body weight per day within the temperature range 20—28°C.

To meet the growth target of 150g during the first summer, the fingerlings must grow at about 2% of their body weight per day over 5 months, and to achieve this they must be fed at the maximum rate consistent with water quality throughout the summer. Commercial channel catfish rations would be adequate but it is worthwhile manufacturing one's own diets, perhaps according to one of the recipes given in the chapter on nutrition. There are many formulations for channel catfish diets in the published literature and a little research will determine what ingredients are available locally at a reasonable price (feed mills are the most convenient supplier in most cases). Samples of the fish from ponds 1 and 2 should be taken at weekly intervals and weighed to assess their progress, feeding rate being altered accordingly.

The Pond Culture of Tilapia

If it were not for their inability to withstand low temperatures, tilapia would be the ideal fish for small-scale culture. They are so undemanding and tolerant of crowded, generally poor environmental conditions that it is difficult to imagine anyone failing to have at least a modicum of success with their farming. As it is, they are certainly the best fish for outdoor culture in tropical climates. Tilapia can be cultured in temperate climates if the culturist is prepared to eat rather small fish, by sacrificing all the stock after one summer, bar a few brood fish. These broodfish are bred in indoor aquaria over the winter and used to provide the next year's seed fish. Unfortunately, this also means that three-quarters of the year's supply of fish must come from preserved stores, either salted, smoked or frozen.

In the introduction, we mentioned the other disadvantages of tilapia culture, that of prolific reproduction. This can be used to advantage in a small farm in temperate climates by producing each year's stock from just a few brood fish, but can be a great problem during the growing season because these fish mature sexually at a very small size. To get fish of a reasonable edible size in just a few months, indiscriminate reproduction must be prevented, and techniques for this are not yet fully reliable or generally available; but to be a pioneer in small-scale tilapia culture may offer more reward than simply producing fish to eat!

We have chosen to describe guidelines for the culture of two species of tilapias, the Java and the Nile Tilapia. Among the hardiest of tilapias, their hybrid offspring are even hardier in some respects than their parents, and both are mouth brooders producing less eggs at a time. This reduces the problem of over-population to some extent. They have slightly different feeding habits, the Java tilapia prefer plankton but adapting to almost anything else, while the Nile tilapia has an ability to consume higher plants, but will eat plankton and farinaceous food. In addition, both these species are available in Europe and the USA as tropical (aquarium) fishes and are not particularly difficult to obtain; in southern parts of the USA, the Java tilapia may be obtainable as a commercially farmed species.

Temperature Requirements
Both Java and Nile tilapia have a lower lethal temperature limit of about 12°C and will begin to grow at temperatures above 15°C. Rapid growth is obtained in the temperature range 20–32°C and the Nile tilapia can survive temperatures as high as 40–42°C for short periods. To obtain reasonable growth therefore, temperatures in the ponds must reach 20°+ and stay there for as long as possible. For this reason it is almost essential to enclose them with a polyethylene greenhouse to get an extra month's growth, unless summers are regularly long.

Growth
Under favourable circumstances, the growth of tilapia can be very rapid, but stunting due to competition with excess young and the retarded growth of females due to frequent reproduction usually bedevils their pond culture. Like carp, there are conflicting opinions as to what constitutes an edible sized tilapia. In a small tilapia pond, operative for five months at most in temperate climates, the largest

fish will weigh little more than 200g and the average size will be about 100g. These, perforce, are edible sized tilapia. Supplementary feeding must be practised at the highest possible rate to achieve good growth, and reproduction must be kept to a minimum. Fry stocked initially after overwintering indoors should be about 4—10cm long and weigh between 8 and 20g.

Pond Facilities

Only one pond is required and this should be of 1.5—2 ares in extent, oblong in shape and covered with a polyethylene greenhouse or a low glass cover. An earth pond is suitable, but care should be taken to make it really watertight. The smaller the inflow to maintain its depth the better. Depth should be between 1 and 1.2m. Venting of the greenhouse is advisable just in case water temperatures rise too much, and there should be a potential inflow of 5 litres per minute above maintenance flow for cooling purposes. It is a good idea to construct the pond below the surrounding ground surface if it can be made drainable, as it will provide slightly more insulation than a dyked pond. Outflow from the pond (if any) should be well screened to prevent ANY escapes, and screens should be no larger than 0.5mm mesh because newly hatched fry are tiny.

The pond should be in an open, sunny preferably south facing position to catch as much sun as possible.

Stocking the Pond

Stocking should begin when water temperatures in the pond have reached at least 15°C, which will probably be about the beginning of May, depending on location. It would be a good idea to purchase a maximum/minimum thermometer and leave this in the pond for three weeks or so before stocking is due to begin. Temperatures are likely to drop sharply at night, despite the buffering capacity of the water, and stocking should not commence until nightly temperatures have reached 15°C every night for a week. If temperatures differ between the pond and the water in the overwintering aquaria (or whatever facility has been used to overwinter the fish), then the tilapia fingerlings should be floated in plastic bags in the pond until temperatures are equilibrated.

The reproduction of Java and Nile tilapia is considered later, together with the production and care of fry for stocking purposes. The mortality of these two species of tilapia is likely to be very low after they have reached a large enough size for stocking the pond, and it will be sufficient to stock the pond with about 200—230 fish. Even with precautions, reproduction will probably occur in the pond during the course of the growing season, and substantially more fish than were originally stocked will be harvested. One female can produce between 70 and 150 eggs per spawning, depending on size, and the majority of these will survive because of the protection afforded by the mouth brooding habit. Sufficient fish for each year's stocking can be easily provided by half a dozen breeding pairs.

There are several methods of limiting overpopulation in the pond, of which two are likely to be of use to the small farmer. Fry can be sexed by hand before release, either males or females being cultured separately although males are usually preferred as their growth is faster and there is little food lost to sexual products. This method is one possibility for the small farm, but requires considerable experience and is unlikely to be completely reliable. It only needs a couple of females to be wrongly sexed and included with the males and all the good work is undone (female Java tilapia are capable of producing broods every six weeks).

The other alternative is to include a predator in with the tilapia population which will selectively crop the smallest fish. Although this is the easiest method, the balance is a delicate one and the results are uncertain. The predator must not grow so swiftly as to outpace the larger fish, but it must keep pace with the fry or else its inclusion will not prove a remedy at all. There are many tropical predators in aquarium shops and some of these might prove suitable. Predaceous fish like these should be stocked with the tilapia at a size just large enough to capture newly-hatched fry. As a general rule, it would not be wise to stock any predator at greater than 4% of the tilapia population to begin with. Some success has been reported when Oscar's or the Velvet Cichlid (Astronotus ocellatus) and the Nile Perch (Lates niloticus) have been used as predators. The slower growing Oscars might be useful as they pose less threat to the larger tilapia. Stocking rates of 2% of the tilapia population for Nile Perch have been recommended as effective.

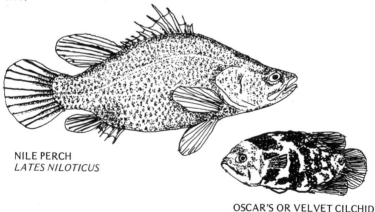

NILE PERCH
LATES NILOTICUS

OSCAR'S OR VELVET CILCHID
ASTRONOTUS OCELLATUS

Fig. 26 **Suitable Predators for use with Tilapia**

Fertilisation

To maximise growth, fertilisation of the backyard tilapia pond is a must. Liming is an important pre-requisite, to provide the neutral or slightly alkaline conditions conducive to good algal and planktonic growth. Inorganic and organic fertilisation both before and while the pond is under water are beneficial provided they are carried out with common sense.

Both species will feed avidly off the plankton produced by successful fertilisation. Superphosphate will be the most effective fertiliser as initial treatment, and should be applied at 1—2kg per are; alternatively, a 1:4:1 mixture of an NPK fertiliser at the same dosage could be applied to the pond bottom before it is put under water. Fertilisation with superphosphate can also be carried out while the pond is stocked, when the algal population has obviously faded, but it should be applied at a much lower rate (about 0.5kg to the are).

Organic fertilisers will encourage the production of Cladocerans like Daphnia, which are particularly attractive to Java tilapia. Two or three kg of animal manure could be applied per week for three weeks out of four, but as always, care should be taken in its application. It would be useful to have a small air compressor of some sort, perhaps a couple of little aquarium air pumps, which could be turned on while manuring and left for twenty four hours or so to safeguard the fish. These would also be useful if temperatures in the pond rise above 30°C, to keep the water well-oxygenated.

Supplementary Feeding

Both species of tilapia are predominantly plankton feeders in the natural state, but both will eat all kinds of artificial feeds of vegetable origin. Java will eat animal food as well, like fish meal, in the absence of vegetable material, while Nile has been suggested as a candidate for aquatic weed control. Both will also readily accept commercial fish pellets, but they prefer to let them fall to the bottom of the pond and break down to some extent — they do learn to take them off the water surface eventually.

It is a good idea to experiment with all the vegetable materials that are to hand, and find out which are liked by the fish. Vegetable tops and peelings should be given in small quantities initially to establish their acceptability. Home made pellets based on soya bean meal would form a good source of protein. Gnats and midges should be encouraged to lay their eggs on the pond, as the larvae are also a good food source. They are easy to attract to the pond with a light and an open window, although they may be a source of discomfort to the culturist. A few commercial pellets will ensure an adequate supply of vitamins and minerals.

What little data there is on suitable feeding rates for tilapia suggests a daily food intake of 3% of the body weight. Because of the likelihood of reproduction in the pond, the standing weight of fish at any one time cannot really be estimated from a sample, as with the other species. It will thus be impossible to feed 3% of the body weight with any accuracy, and it will have to suffice to feed as much as the fish can apparently eat in a day. Frequent feeding, at least during the first few weeks, will give some indication of this amount and will help the fish to grow more quickly. Bunches of leaves should be suspended in the pond and withdrawn after a few hours to check whether they have been eaten. If all the leaves have been stripped from the stems, another bunch should be supplied. With pellets, it will be more difficult to gauge how well the fish are feeding. If temperatures are high enough (above 22°C), the fish will take pellets from the surface sometimes and the feeding response can then be seen easily. A rough idea of the total fish weight in the pond can be gained by weighing a sample of the largest fish, and working out the total weight according to the number stocked. The total weight of food distributed in one day should not then exceed 5—6% of this weight, unless it contains a great deal of water. This will at least give an inaccurate upper limit.

Harvesting

As soon as any tilapia appear to be of a suitable size for eating, cropping can commence. It is difficult to say when this is likely to be, because the growth of fish under culture conditions is very variable. Certainly male tilapia of both species will be the first edible sized fish, as their growth will be two or three times as rapid as the females. This is largely due to the mouth incubating habit of the species, for the female will not eat for 15—20 days while she is caring for young.

When the temperatures in the pond begin to fall, probably at the beginning of October, the pond should be drained (with great care, to prevent any escapes) and all the fish harvested. Those too small to be eaten could be used as chicken feed. Six males and females should be transferred to a winter breeding facility (whose design and construction is dealt with in the chapter on reproduction) to provide the young fish for the following year's operation, while the rest are dressed and either frozen or preserved in some other way. Dressing loss for each fish will be about 45—50%. Bear in mind that most freezers can only store fish for six months; the rest of the year's supply will probably have to come from salted reserves. Fresh tilapia are widely held to be one of the most delicious of fish.

6 water recycling systems

Ponds have their uses; but below a certain size, their output becomes an occasional luxury rather than a regular contribution to food supplies. The garden of an average town house is rarely large enough for more than the cultivation of some vegetables and perhaps the keeping of a few chickens. It is not the place for dykes and drainage ditches. If we want to keep fish in a restricted area and in quantities comparable with the output of ponds, then we must choose an efficient, space-saving method of doing so. A recycling system can be a suitable technique for fish rearing in these circumstances.

It has long been known that running water has a beneficial effect on the growth and health of fish, due to the continuous elimination of toxic substances and the replenishment of dissolved oxygen, but that is not all that is required of a recycling system. The water must also be of good quality. Aquatic animals have always to live among their own excrement, and maintenance of water quality depends on the continual removal of this. Simple filtration cannot remove soluble toxins like ammonia, so other treatment is required in addition. Sewage disposal and water filtration have become complex sciences, but a recycling system embodies the oldest principle of waterborne waste treatment, that of bacterial degradation. The biological filter of a recirculating system is really a 'bacteria house', which provides ideal surroundings for the growth and proliferation of the bacteria that break down solid and soluble waste. By concentrating them in one place, the filter promotes interaction of all the different types of bacteria, and effectively speeds up their natural biological action. It also acts as a mechanical filter, removing suspended solids from the water. It is thus a very important part of a recycling system.

Quite apart from their high productivity despite small physical size, recycling systems embrace energy and resource conservation with a degree of adaptability unequalled by other fish husbandry systems. By reducing the fish to water ratio from something like 1:20,000 in ponds to 1:100 or less, much greater control over the fish is possible, together with rationalisation of water use.

Virtually autonomous water requirements mean that recirculating systems can be located almost anywhere and the choice of species cultured in indoor systems is not limited by the vagaries of climate. A well-insulated warm water recycling system minimises heat losses and makes artificial heating economical, especially as the design of such systems integrates well with alternative energy sources like wind pumps and solar panels. They have the least environmental impact of any intensive form of fish farming, and can be operated in conjunction with agricultural, hydroponic and similar projects.

The capital investment required for a recycling system is greater than that for a pond, which is why their size is usually limited. There is no reason why recycling systems should not be made very large; their productivity would certainly justify the initial outlay if they were well managed, but careful design and pilot-scale experimentation would be required before theory could become reality.

Although recycling systems can vary greatly in design, they have in common three basic elements; tanks for holding the fish, a water filter and a recirculating pump. In practice, two other components are often included, a settling tank for removing the bulk of suspended solids and a header tank for evening out the water supply to the holding tanks. The pump transfers the water draining from the filter to the header tank, which supplies water to the fish tanks. These drain back to the filter via the settling tank, and the whole cycle is repeated.

Each of these five components will be considered in turn before

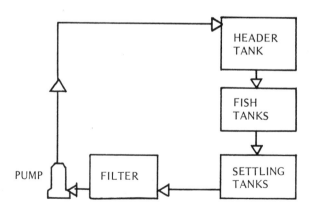

Fig. 27 **Cycle of Operation**

we discuss the building of an actual system, because it is important to understand how the design of one part can affect all the others. By far the most vital part of a system is the biological filter. The health (and life!) of the fish depends entirely on the continuing efficient functioning of this installation. In turn, the filter can only operate within the limits of its construction and it is often forgotten that the filter bed is just as much a living structure and dependent on environmental conditions as are the fish in the tanks. It is composed of countless interacting bacteria, protozoa and other creatures. An appreciation of some of the processes that take place in a filter bed and the way these are influenced by external factors is essential if the culturist is to get the most out of a recycling system.

The Filter Bed

We advocate biological filters for the farm because they are the simplest means of maintaining water quality. There are other methods of filtration but they are all comparatively expensive and more difficult to look after. Biological filters themselves can vary considerably in design, but their purpose and mechanism of operation are identical. All have in common a mixed population of bacteria whose joint action breaks down the organic and inorganic wastes liberated by the fish. These wastes may be solid or soluble and the filter must be able to cope with both types.

It has been explained that the principal soluble waste product of fish was ammonia excreted by the gills. In addition, small amounts of other substances like urea are released, but these rarely build up to hazardous levels. All these wastes are end products of nitrogen metabolism, and represent a way the fish can dispose of nitrogen quite safely under normal circumstances. However, a recycling system does not constitute 'normal circumstances', for its water does not offer an infinite diluting capacity. Decomposition of faeces and uneaten food allowed to remain in the system also tends to release such bound nitrogen as toxins like ammonia. It is evident, therefore, that the most important action of a biological filter is the conversion of harmful nitrogenous compounds, principally ammonia, to less poisonous substances.

These harmless forms are nitrate and free nitrogen, predominantly nitrate. The formation of nitrate in a biological filter is associated with two species of bacteria, *Nitrosomas* and *Nitrobacter*. In the presence of oxygen, *Nitrosomas* converts ammonia to nitrite, which is then oxidised to nitrate by *Nitrobacter*. The presence of oxygen is essential for these vital reactions to occur unhindered, and the filter must be constructed so as to ensure adequate oxygenation at all times. If these reactions should be slowed or stopped by an absence of oxygen, ammonia will quickly build up to dangerous levels and threaten the fish. Other factors such as pH and temperature affect nitrate formation to a lesser extent.

Many other species of bacteria, collectively called *heterotrophic bacteria*, are involved in waste decomposition. *Nitrosomas* and *Nitrobacter* belong to a special group called *autotrophic bacteria* which 'feed' on simpler nitrogen compounds than the heterotrophs.

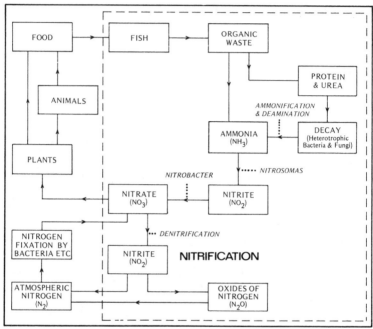

Those events within the dashed lines occur within a recycling system. They are only a part of the total nitrogen cycle.

Fig. 28 **The Nitrogen Cycle in Relation to Recycling Systems**

Since the rate of removal of ammonia and other toxins will be proportional to the absolute numbers of bacteria present in the filter bed, it is evident that the greater the surface area of the filter bed material, the more bacteria there will be in that bed. For this reason, filters are usually constructed of gravel and/or crushed shells, because these substances have a large surface area compared with their volume. Angular gravel will be more effective than rounded, smooth pebbles. There is a lower limit to the size of gravel employed, below which clogging problems are encountered.

Because the bacteria remove oxygen from the water as it passes them, there will be progressively less dissolved oxygen in successive depths of a flooded filter bed. Consequently, it is better to have a filter that has a large surface area, and is relatively shallow, than one that is tall and narrow.

TYPES OF BIOLOGICAL FILTER

All biological filters have in common the biological oxidation of wastes, but some in addition to this function serve as mechanical filters to a greater or lesser extent. For example, the sand filters sometimes used during sewage processing have a nitrifying capacity, but are used to clarify the effluent before it is discharged in to a water course. There are three types of filter popular for treating fish farm effluent:

Submerged Filters
These are simple to construct and therefore commonly used. They consist of a shallow tank containing the filter medium (gravel, anthracite, limestone etc.) supported on a perforated filter plate. The filter medium is at all times flooded, and water can flow either up or down through the filter, most frequently down. To maintain oxygenation throughout the bed, water is pumped through at a fairly high flow rate and any cessation of this pumping causes anaerobic bacteria to

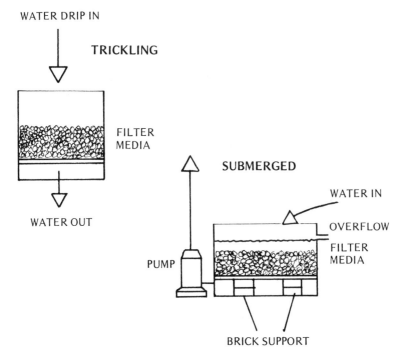

Fig. 29 **Types of Biological Filter**

proliferate. Although this type of filter is well able to cope with the demands made of it, it does have several drawbacks. The first is need for continuous water flow; if sedimentation is inefficient, organic matter deposits on the surface of the filter to form a mat, which slows down the flow and causes 'ponding'. Water flows through the regions of least resistance and only a small proportion of the filter volume is then actively concerned with nitrification. Larger filter media avoid this problem to some extent, but reduce the number of surfaces for bacterial attachment. Gravel of 2–5mm diameter has been recommended as the minimum workable size for filters of this type. Because submerged gravel filters can cope with the relatively high flow rate used in our recycling system, we have opted to use these, but the following types all have application in fish farming.

Trickling Filters
These are well able to cope with high pollutional loadings but only have a low throughput of water. The advantage of these filters is their good oxygenation at all levels. The filter water exists as a film over the surface of the filter media, the interstices through the rest of the bed containing air. The diffusion of oxygen into the water therefore occurs throughout the whole filter bed. In contrast to the submerged filters, water drains through them under the action of gravity.

Activated Sludge Filters
These filters essentially consist of the heterotrophic and autotrophic bacteria without media for attachment. Although systems such as these have been shown to be potentially useful for commercial fish culture, they require a great deal of attention and equipment.

Factors affecting the Operation of Filters
Apart from dissolved oxygen, other factors are important for the efficient operation of a filter bed.
Temperature
The overall optimum temperature for the growth of nitrifying bacteria appears to be in the range 28–36°C, so that conversion of ammonia to nitrate will proceed more rapidly as temperatures increase. A warm water recycling system containing carp, for example, is theoretically able to cope with a higher level of ammonia for a given filter area than a cold water system containing trout.
pH
The pH plays a very important part in the filter. When a filter is first put into operation, the bacterial population takes some time to establish itself and in the meantime certain end products of metabolism accumulate. Ammonia accumulates first, and reaches a peak after a few days as the population of *Nitrosomas* increases. As ammonia concentration falls, nitrite builds up until *Nitrobacter* can oxidise it to

nitrate. Both ammonia and nitrite are highly toxic to fish. The toxicity of ammonia is pH dependent, and a falling pH increases the proportion of ionised ammonia which is less toxic to fish. Nitrite concentrations above 0.4ppm are toxic and above 0.012ppm it is thought to inhibit growth. There is a conflict between the requirements of the nitrifying bacteria which have an optimal pH range of 7.5–8 and the nitrate-removing bacteria which require a pH of less than 7. The pH linked toxicity of ammonia complicates this problem; at $25^{\circ}C$ and a pH of 8 a total ammonia level of 0.47ppm is considered safe. At pH 7 this can be increased to 4.4ppm and at pH 6 to 44.5ppm. However, the total amount of unionised ammonia should always be kept below 0.01ppm to ensure the health of the fish, and we will return to this point at a later stage (see table 10). A compromise must be struck with pH to promote good nitrification, denitrification and to minimise ammonia toxicity. The most desirable pH range is 7 to 7.5. The accumulation of nitrate tends to acidify the water, and buffering capacity is necessary to oppose this change in pH. The usual method of pH regulation is to include materials like crushed oyster shell, dolomite or limestone in the filter, although some doubt has been expressed as to their long-term efficacy.

Excess build up of nitrate is also undesirable, but a reasonable inflow of freshwater into the recycling system (1–2% of the system volume per day) usually keeps nitrate at an acceptable level.

The Performance of Biological Filters

The oxidation of ammonia to nitrate is critical to the successful operation of recycling systems. The rate of ammonia production by the fish depends on the amount of nitrogen containing food given to them, above a baseline amount, while the nitrification rate depends on the number of nitrifying bacteria in the filter bed. These rates partially determine the carrying capacity, or the total number of organisms that can safely be held in a system, together with the oxygen removing and generating capacity of the system. When a system is stocked below its carrying capacity an equilibrium is established between production/oxidation resulting in no accumulation of ammonia or nitrite. It is always desirable to reach an equilibrium state, but to achieve this requires some knowledge of the carrying capacity.

Even though we can arrive at a very crude figure for the carrying capacity based on a number of assumptions, it is very important to evaluate practically the capabilities of a system while it is working, and to gradually increase its loading until a steady state is arrived at which gives a good margin of error.

We will consider how to estimate the capacity of a system after we have discussed the other components of a recycling system.

Sedimentation Tanks

Build up of organic matter — fish faeces and food residues — has a deleterious effect on the operation of a filter. It can clog the spaces between the filter media, causing local deoxygenation and an uneven flow through the filter bed, or simply overload the filter's ability to cope with ammonia. It also favours the development of heterotrophic bacteria with a reduction in the rate of nitrification.

Conveniently, fish faeces under culture conditions usually take the form of discrete pellets surrounded by a mucous membrane, which are easy to settle out and remove from the system, but there is also a considerable amount of finely divided suspended matter in the water. It exists at a low concentration, but is not negligible and may interfere with the fishes' breathing and dispose them towards gill diseases. Because of its size and low concentration, it is difficult to remove from the water and a sedimentation facility must be fairly efficient.

The simplest type of sedimentation basin consists of a tank through which the water from the fish tanks passes on its way to the filter. The reduction in water velocity achieved by exit from a small diameter pipe into a relatively large volume allows heavier particles to settle to the bottom of the tank, under the action of gravity, from where they may be removed by syphon or by drainage. Very small, light particles will not settle unless the sedimentation basin is very large and the water velocity close to zero, which it cannot be in a confined space.

The key to successful sedimentation is the reduction in flow rate through the sedimentation tank, and this must be as great as possible. The longer that the water can be retained in the facility, the more chance it will have to clarify. Distributing the water flow throughout the whole tank volume will cause an overall reduction in water

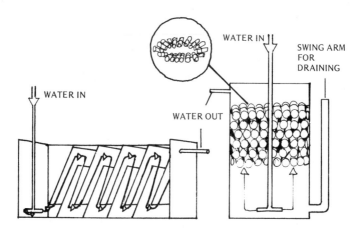

Fig. 30 **Sedimentation Tanks**

velocity through the tank greater than that caused by a single inflow and outflow. This distribution can be effected by regularly spaced plates or bundles of pipework placed in the tank to divert the flow. It also gives a greatly increased surface area for particles to settle out and be entrained upon.

The baffles in the sedimentation tank should be fixed together in such a way as to make it possible to lift the complete assembly out of the water for cleaning. Bundles of pipe can be tied or wired together. It is better to have the pipes or plates pointing down towards the bottom of the tank in order that the settled waste may fall to the bottom. A perforated pipe on the inflow extending the whole width of the tank will help to distribute the water flow through the tank, and reduce the tendency to 'stream' — to have a localised region of fast water flow.

The sludge that collects in the bottom of a sedimentation tank makes an excellent fertiliser.

THE FISH TANKS

These are considerably simpler in design than anything we have talked about so far. They may be constructed of a host of materials such as glass fibre, concrete, corrugated iron, plastic or wood, as long as they are durable, hold water and fish. If the tanks are raised off the ground, adequate support must be supplied because water is very heavy — 1000 litres of water weighs a tonne!

Circular tanks are best from the point of view of cleaning, and glass fibre ones can be built at home, using a wooden mould, but it is not a very pleasant task. Ready-made glass fibre tanks designed for other purposes (e.g. chemical treatment baths, waste bins and the like) are perfectly good and considerably cheaper than purpose built fibreglass tanks for fish farming. Their only disadvantage is that they tend to come in square or oblong shapes. New glass fibre tanks should be washed thoroughly before they are stocked with fish, because some of the solvents tend to linger in the fibreglass and leach out into the water initially. It is best to fill them with water and leave a hosepipe running into them for a couple of days at least before putting them into service.

A single large tank set into the ground would probably best be built from concrete, but remember to put in all the pipework before pouring the concrete. All the plumbing in any recycling system should preferably be made of a non-toxic plastic. The materials in recycled water tend to dissolve conventional piping made of copper, which is very toxic to the fish. For the same reason, if galvanised corrugated iron is used to build tanks, it should be carefully painted at all points in contact with the water with a non-toxic waterproof paint (at least three coats) to prevent the zinc going into solution. Untreated galvanised iron is all right for outdoor tanks with a throughflow of water, because the zinc never has chance to accumulate.

Header Tanks

Whether a header tank is used or not will depend on the design of the system. Any type of tank will do, probably the best being a plastic cold water header tank used in conventional house plumbing. These are usually readily available from plumber's merchants at a reasonable cost.

A header tank is useful not only for evening out the water flow to the fish tanks, but as a secondary sedimentation tank (it is surprising just how much muck collects in a header tank!) and an oxygenating facility. Water pumped up to the header tank can be caused to fall over a series of baffles into the tank, which spreads it thin and enhances oxygen diffusion.

Pumps

Although the filter is responsible for the purification of the water passing through it, the volume of water moving around the system is dependent on the capacity of the pump and it is this that essentially determines how many fish can be kept in a system. In moving water from one part of the system to another, the pump effects water purification and reoxygenation, and the flow rate of water through the tanks determines to a large extent how many fish can be held in them. It is also the weak link in the system, the thing most likely to go wrong, and for this reason it should be chosen carefully.

There are many different water pumps for sale, some more efficient than others. We would advocate the use of submersible water pumps, especially when recycling systems are operated at elevated temperatures, because they then approach 100% efficiency as heat generated by the pump is tranferred to the water. Submersible pumps are also among the most rugged and reliable types available and can be used with a minimum of maintenance.

We have designed our recycling system around a pump capable of delivering 70 litres of water/minute to a height (head) of 3 metres. Some of the better submersible pumps with a power rating of about 150 watts can put out 100 litres of water to this height quite comfortably and this is the type to get. The cost of pumping in the economics of recycling systems is a considerable one, so it is important to choose a pump which will meet the water requirement for a minimum energy expenditure.

It is worth considering the use of a wind generator to power an electric pump in more isolated installations, and using a battery storage system to even out the power fluctuation. Many designs for home-made wind generators from 'spare parts' are available, and some would undoubtedly meet the needs of a small recycling system.

Although home-made windmills are not too expensive to construct, the battery storage arrangement is. Even in the most favourable locations, sufficient storage is required to supply at least three days' power in the event of a calm, and this involves a lot of batteries.

Oxygenating Equipment

As oxygen is removed from the system by its living components, so must it be put back if the water is to be fit for re-use. There are various means of improving the transfer of oxygen from the air into the water, and one or two we have already mentioned. For example, jetting water into tanks entrains some air with the water flow, and improves oxygen diffusion, as does spreading the water thin over a plate or series of baffles, increasing the surface area of contact between the liquid and gaseous phases.

Although we have not included more sophisticated methods of oxgenation in the practical design of our system, there is a simple device which is very efficient at improving oxygen transfer. This is the venturi.

Venturi Oxygenation

A venturi is simply a constriction in a pipe with an opening to the air, and the basic principle is illustrated in fig. 31. Reducing the diameter of a pipe increases the water pressure, and in a venturi, the pressurised flow is allowed to expand into a chamber past the constriction. This creates a vacuum by the air inlet, and air is drawn in to mix with the water. The trapped bubbles move along with the water flow and some oxygen diffusion occurs before the water is discharged from the pipe. A venturi would ideally be inserted in the pipe containing water from the pump on its way to the header tank, so that treated water is then passed directly to the fish tanks.

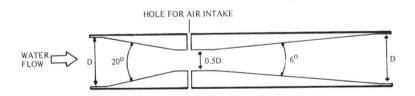

Fig. 31   **Cross-section of Venturi Constriction in a Water Pipe**

DESIGNING A RECYCLING SYSTEM

Rather than deal with recycling systems for each of the four species separately, as we did with ponds, we will describe one basic system and modifications of it to suit the needs of each species where these are divergent.

Unlike a pond, a recycling system is run on a continuous basis without fallow periods or annual restockings, and this requires a radically different approach to husbandry. The carrying capacity, or the total number of fish that can be held in a system at one time, is smaller than that of a series of ponds because of the reduction in overall water volume, even though the stocking density may be higher. To produce the same weight of fish in a comparable time, it is thus necessary to adopt a strategy of continuous stocking and culling as far as possible, maintaining an approximately constant weight of fish in the system at all times. Such a husbandry scheme uses the potential of a recycling system to the full, but makes management a slightly more complicated affair than pond farming.

The Concept of Carrying Capacity

The carrying capacity of a recycling system is simply the maximum weight of fish that it is capable of holding, above which its purification facilities cannot maintain the water quality at a standard compatible with the health of the animals. The carrying capacity is affected by the species of fish, the system's operating temperature, the water make-up and the rate of feeding, but above all the rate of water turnover in the system. It is a balance between those factors tending to improve water quality and those causing deterioration.

The rate of water turnover is directly linked to the oxygen generating capacity of a recycling system and it is this which is likely to be the first limiting factor determining the stocking density, the actual number of fish held in the system. This must always be below the carrying capacity to allow a safe margin of error. Fish, the filter and food residues remove oxygen from the water and the combined amount that they remove must always be less than the amount put back into the system.

Numerically, the stocking density is usually expressed in one of three ways:

1) As Number or weight of fish/unit surface area of container (e.g. kg/m^2)
2) As Number or weight of fish/unit volume of container e.g. kg/m^3)
or 3) As number or weight of fish/unit volume of inflow into the container (e.g. kg/litre/minute)

where a container may be a pond or a fishtank. The first term is frequently applied to extensive culture in ponds, where the stocking density is usually low and the amount of natural food available to the fish is proportional to the area of the pond bottom. Terms 2) and 3) are the most common expressions of stocking density, but it is better to take into account both the inflow to and the volume of a fish compound when considering practical stocking densities.

Oxygen Demands of Fish

In simple terms, oxygen is removed from the water by fish as it is needed to oxidise food to produce energy. Broadly speaking, the oxygen consumption of a fish increases as the food intake, its activity and the water temperature increase. However, when expressed as a percentage of a fixed fish weight, oxygen consumption decreases as the fish grow (i.e. 1kg of large fish require less oxygen than 1kg of small fish).

There comes a point at which the dissolved oxygen level is so low that the fish cannot obtain it rapidly enough to meet their requirements, this lower limit varying to a certain extent with species. For rainbow trout and catfish it is about 5ppm and for carp and tilapia, around 3ppm. On no account should the level of dissolved oxygen in the water of a recycling system (or a pond, for that matter) fall below these levels. Table 9 shows the oxygen content of water at differing temperatures, and it is easy to see how small is the difference between 100% saturation and the lower critical limits at higher temperatures.

The difference between the level of oxygen in saturated water of a particular temperature and the minimum safe level for a fish species is the amount of oxygen available to the fish for its bodily needs. Thus, for rainbow trout in water at 16°C, the amount of available oxygen is 10.0 (the number of mg/litre of oxygen in saturated water of this temperature from table 9) − 5 = 5ppm.

Unfed fish consume a certain amount of oxygen, the amount depending on whether the fish is actively swimming or merely remaining stationary in a current of water. The latter or routine metabolic requirement is the lowest normal level, and fish in the actively swimming state or in a state of stress may consume up to three times the routine metabolic oxygen requirement. The routine metabolic oxygen requirement also varies with the size of the fish, and as yet it has been poorly investigated for different fish species. What data there is suggests the routine requirement is in the region of 100mg of oxygen/kg of fish/hour for small (100g) fish of the majority of species. Smaller fish require more oxygen, and larger fish less. In a recycling system, this would be the average consumption of the fish provided they were infrequently disturbed and general water quality remained good.

On top of this oxygen requirement comes that needed to metabolise ingested food. This is highly variable, depending on the quality of the food, and very difficult to measure. One commercial trout food has been reported as requiring 90g of oxygen for the metabolism of 1kg of ingested pellets, but diets containing high fat levels would probably require more than this. We will assume a figure of 100g/kg of food as a reasonable approximation.

Oxygen Demands of Filters

Based on the chemical reaction for the oxidation of ammonia to nitrate, 3.77g of oxygen are needed for every 1g of ammonia oxidised to nitrate, which gives an absolute minimum requirement for the

Table 9 The Oxygen Content of Water at Various Temperatures and Percentages of Saturation. Oxygen in mgs/litre (ppm).

Temp.	Percentage Saturation						
°C	100	95	90	85	80	75	70
1	14.2	13.5	12.8	12.1	11.4	10.7	9.9
2	13.8	13.1	12.4	11.7	11.0	10.4	9.7
3	13.5	12.8	12.2	11.5	10.8	10.1	9.5
4	13.1	12.4	11.8	11.1	10.5	9.8	9.2
5	12.8	12.2	11.5	10.9	10.2	9.6	9.0
6	12.5	11.9	11.3	10.6	10.0	9.4	8.8
7	12.2	11.6	11.0	10.4	9.8	9.2	8.5
8	11.9	11.3	10.7	10.1	9.5	8.9	8.3
9	11.6	11.0	10.4	9.9	9.3	8.7	8.1
10	11.3	10.7	10.2	9.6	9.0	8.5	7.9
11	11.1	10.5	10.0	9.4	8.9	8.3	7.8
12	10.8	10.3	9.7	9.2	8.6	8.1	7.6
13	10.6	10.1	9.5	9.0	8.5	8.0	7.4
14	10.4	9.9	9.4	8.8	8.3	7.8	7.3
15	10.2	9.7	9.2	8.7	8.2	7.7	7.1
16	10.0	9.5	9.0	8.5	8.0	7.5	7.0
17	9.7	9.2	8.7	8.2	7.8	7.3	6.8
18	9.5	9.0	8.6	8.1	7.6	7.1	6.7
19	9.4	8.9	8.5	8.0	7.5	7.1	6.6
20	9.2	8.7	8.3	7.8	7.4	6.9	6.4
21	9.0	8.6	8.1	7.7	7.2	6.8	6.3
22	8.8	8.4	7.9	7.5	7.0	6.6	6.2
23	8.7	8.3	7.8	7.4	6.9	6.5	6.1
24	8.5	8.1	7.7	7.2	6.8	6.4	6.0
25	8.4	8.0	7.6	7.1	6.7	6.3	5.9
26	8.2	7.8	7.4	7.0	6.6	6.2	5.7
27	8.0	7.6	7.2	6.8	6.4	6.0	5.6
28	7.9	7.5	7.1	6.7	6.3	5.9	5.5
29	7.8	7.4	7.0	6.6	6.2	5.8	5.5
30	7.6	7.2	6.8	6.5	6.0	5.7	5.3

oxygen demands of the filter when the rate of ammonia production by the fish is known. It allows no metabolic rate for any of the bacteria within the filter, so some correction must be made for this.

The majority of oxygen required by the filter will be used for the oxidation of ammonia, since this is the principal waste product of fish. The rate of ammonia production by the fish is dependent, like the oxygen requirement, on the rate of feeding above a background level, but fish fed at 2% of their body weight per day would result in a minimum filter requirement of 125mg of oxygen/kg of fish/hour.

In practice, the oxygen requirement of the filter would be more than this and some studies suggest around 150mg of oxygen/kg of fish/ hour as the requirement. Some other studies suggest oxygen consumption during filtration to be about twice this value, but they take into account pollution from faeces and uneaten food, which we will consider separately.

Other Oxygen Demands
Both suspended solids and settled organic matter tend to remove oxygen from the water, the amount depending on their accumulation. This is why it is important to remove suspended solids via a sedimentation basin as far as possible, and to remove the settled material frequently. The oxygen demand of such organic matter is measured in terms of the Biochemical Oxygen Demand (BOD), or the oxygen required to metabolise the waste. A BOD of 10mg/litre (or 10ppm) simply means each litre of waste requires 10mg of oxygen for its purification.

The volume of organic wastes will depend on the number of fish in a system, the rate of feeding and the type of food. Diets high in fibre will be less completely digested and will result in the fish producing a greater volume of faeces, and some dietary ingredients cause rapid disintegration of faeces which leads to more suspended matter in the water. Suspended matter will require the greater quantity of dissolved oxygen because of its enormous surface area, while settled matter will only remove oxygen from the water in its immediate vicinity.

Typical values for the oxygen requirement of fish farm effluent range from 200—500mg of oxygen/kg of fish/hour. When this amount is added to the oxygen requirements of the filter and the fish, it can be seen that a considerable amount of oxygen is removed from the water in a recycling system every hour, and the same amount must be replaced in this time.

Estimating the Carrying Capacity
We will assume that the pumping arrangement of the recycling system is capable of delivering a reasonably constant flow rate of 70 litres per minute to the fish holding facility. Whether it is split between two or more fish tanks will not affect the overall carrying capacity of the system to an appreciable extent, and we are now in a position to quantify the carrying capacity.

We will also assume that the reoxygenating capacity of the system, essentially effected during the circuit of the water from the filter back to the fish tanks, is capable of returning water at 50% saturation back to 85% saturation. This means that 70 litres of water at 85% or more saturation is available per minute, which should be well within the abilities of the system we will describe, the actual amount of oxygen in weight terms dissolved in the water depending on the operating temperature of the system.

In a system containing rainbow trout, and at a temperature of 12°C, the amount of available oxygen in each litre of water is (9.2 - 5) = 4.2mg. The total amount of available oxygen per hour is thus (4.2 x 70 x 60) = 17.64g.

The routine metabolic requirement of 1kg of fish we will take as 100mg/hour, and to this must be added the oxygen required for the metabolism of ingested food. If they were fed at a rate of 2% of their body weight per day, and we take the value of 100g of oxygen per kg of food, then the total oxygen requirement of the fish is about $(100 + (\frac{100 \times 20}{24})) = 185$mg/kg of fish/hour.

If we take the value for the oxygen demands of the filter as 150mg/kg of fish/hour, and the intermediate value for the oxygen demands of settled and suspended organic matter (350mg/kg of fish/hour), and add these to the oxygen requirement of the fish, we arrive at a total oxygen requirement for the system of 685mg of oxygen/kg of fish/hour.

Since the rate of supply of oxygen is equal to 17640mg/hour, we are left with 16955mg of usable oxygen per hour. The carrying capacity of the system is thus approximately (17640/685) = 26kg of rainbow trout at a water temperature of 12°C, and a feeding rate of 2% of the body weight per day.

If the temperature of the system were to be increased to 16°C, our upper recommended limit for trout, the amount of available oxygen per hour is reduced to (3.5 x 70 x 60) = 14700mg per hour, and the carrying capacity is correspondingly reduced to about 21kg. At lower temperatures, the carrying capacity is increased, and so on.

This method of estimating the carrying capacity of a recycling system is rather crude, but it does give an idea of the capabilities of a system. However, it is very important to determine practically the ability of a system to cope with different fish densities by gradually increasing the stocking density until the point where problems begin to appear. If the stocking density is then kept just below this point, the system will be working at capacity. In the beginning, it is better to underestimate the potential of a system by using the calculations shown above, and thus avoid creating problems which cannot be dealt with satisfactorily. As with pond farming, experience familiarises one with a system and it is possible to diagnose problems at an early stage before they represent a threat.

It is possible to use the same information to estimate the carrying capacity of ponds, or the amount of food that may be safely distributed. For example, a pond containing 10kg of trout in water of 16°C, and fed at 2% of their body weight per day, weill require a certain inflow to meet its oxygen requirements. If the inflowing water is 90%

saturated, and we again take the value of 100mg of oxygen for every gram of ingested food, the water contains 4mg/litre available oxygen and the requirement for the food is 20,000mg per day. A quick estimate for the routine metabolic oxygen requirement of the fish can be made by adding 50% to this latter figure, so the total oxygen requirement per day is 20,000 x 1.5 = 30,000mg per day. The inflow required to supply 30,000mg/day of usable oxygen is thus (30,000/4 = 7500 litres/day) or (7500/1440) = 5.2 litres/minute.

Ammonia

After oxygen, ammonia build-up is likely to be the second limiting factor on the carrying capacity of a system. Temperature and pH govern the proportion of unionised ammonia in the water for a given concentration of total ammonia, which is the parameter most easily measured. We mentioned previously that it is advisable to keep the level of unionised ammonia below 0.01ppm at all times, to prevent it exerting an inhibiting effect on growth, and table 10 shows the permissible amount of total ammonia in water of differing pH and temperature which will maintain unionised ammonia below this level. In ponds, an inflow sufficient to meet the respiratory requirements of the fish is usually sufficient to eliminate ammonia before it can build up to dangerous levels while the action of the filter in a recycling system may sometimes not be able to do this. The level of ammonia production by the fish depends on the level of feeding and on average, 1g of diet would result in the production of 40mg of ammonia. At a level of feeding of 2% of the body weight per day, the ammonia output would therefore be about 33mg/kg of fish/hour. It can be seen that increasing the rate of feeding will reduce the carrying capacity of the system further.

Ammonia and oxygen levels in the water can be measured by chemical methods or by electronic meters. The former are rather time consuming and fiddly, but do have a considerable cost advantage over meters. We would suggest an investment in an oxygen meter, facilitating rapid and routine checks, as this is the most important water quality parameter.

The Volume Requirement of Recycling Systems

The species considered in this book are all quite tolerant of crowded conditions, that is large numbers or weights of fish per unit volume of water. For trout the normal load is usually in the region of $30-60kg/m^3$ and $95-130kg/m^3$ for catfish, carp and tilapia. We would recommend these as maximum stocking densities.

Overall, the space requirement of fish is small when expressed as a weight per unit volume, mainly because most culture tanks are considerably larger than the individual volume requirement giving a single fish plenty of room to move around. Overstocking, from the behavioural

Table 10 Maximum Permissible Total Ammonia Levels at Various Temperatures and pH Values.

(Ammonia Levels expressed as mgs/litre)

pH	\(^{\circ}C\) Temperature										
	6	8	10	12	14	16	18	20	22	24	26
6.0	73.5	62.9	53.8	45.9	39.4	33.9	29.2	25.2	21.8	18.9	16.6
6.2	46.5	39.7	33.9	29.0	24.9	21.4	18.4	15.9	13.8	11.9	10.3
6.4	29.4	25.0	21.4	18.3	15.7	13.5	11.6	10.0	8.70	7.52	6.54
6.6	18.6	15.8	13.5	11.5	9.90	8.55	7.35	6.33	5.46	4.74	4.13
6.8	11.7	10.0	8.55	7.30	6.25	5.38	4.63	4.00	3.46	3.00	2.60
7.0	7.4	6.29	5.38	4.61	3.95	3.40	2.92	2.53	2.19	1.90	1.65
7.2	4.7	3.97	3.40	2.91	2.49	2.15	1.85	1.60	1.38	1.20	1.04
7.4	2.9	2.51	2.15	1.84	1.58	1.36	1.17	1.01	0.88	0.76	0.66
7.6	1.86	1.59	1.36	1.16	1.00	0.86	0.74	0.64	0.56	0.48	0.42
7.8	1.18	1.01	0.86	0.74	0.63	0.55	0.47	0.41	0.35	0.31	0.27
8.0	0.75	0.64	0.55	0.47	0.40	0.35	0.30	0.26	0.23	0.20	0.17
8.2	0.48	0.41	0.35	0.30	0.26	0.22	0.19	0.17	0.15	0.13	0.11
8.4	0.30	0.26	0.22	0.19	0.17	0.14	0.13	0.11	0.097	0.085	0.075
8.6	0.20	0.17	0.14	0.13	0.11	0.095	0.083	0.073	0.065	0.057	0.051
8.8	0.13	0.11	0.095	0.083	0.072	0.064	0.056	0.050	0.044	0.040	0.036
9.0	0.084	0.073	0.064	0.056	0.050	0.044	0.039	0.035	0.032	0.029	0.026
9.2	0.056	0.050	0.044	0.039	0.035	0.031	0.028	0.026	0.024	0.022	0.020
9.4	0.039	0.035	0.031	0.028	0.026	0.023	0.022	0.020	0.019	0.018	0.017
9.6	0.028	0.026	0.023	0.022	0.020	0.019	0.017	0.016	0.015	0.015	0.014
9.8	0.022	0.020	0.019	0.017	0.016	0.015	0.014	0.014	0.013	0.013	0.013
10.0	0.017	0.016	0.015	0.015	0.014	0.013	0.013	0.013	0.012	0.012	0.012

point of view, can lead to aggression between the fish, even with docile species such as carp. Rainbow trout are especially prone to fin nipping, which leads to secondary infections. A similar problem can be encountered with understocking, again most frequently with trout. More dominant fish try to appropriate more space for themselves, behaviour which is suppressed in more crowded conditions.

There is thus an intermediate stocking density which avoids such problems, but this can be affected by tank characteristics (shape, depth, colour, water flow dynamics, amount of light etc) and is peculiar to a particular system. It can only be determined by trial and error.

7 a practical system

Siting

Siting will largely be dependent on available space, but trout systems can be either indoors or out, while catfish, carp and tilapia systems are better placed indoors for temperature conservation purposes. A garage or similar outbuilding would generally be more than adequate for a medium-sized system, and with a suitable aspect, would also provide a good site for mounting solar panels.

The system we will describe has a floor space requirement of about 7 square metres and operates with a continuous pumping rate of 70 litres/minute. The filter is of the submerged gravel type, and the sedimentation basin is similar to the one described previously. It is suitable for keeping all the species, and we will describe how to adapt it to the needs of each.

Components of the System

We suggest the use of three identical circular tanks for keeping the fish, each being about 1 metre in diameter, 0.75 metres deep and containing water to a depth of 0.5 metres. The total water volume of the tanks is thus about 1200 litres or just over 1 cubic metre. The filter tank and the sedimentation basin are the same size, about 2 metres long by 1 metre wide and 0.5 metres deep, each containing 1 cubic metre of water. A header tank about 0.75 metres long by 0.50 metres wide by 0.75 metres deep and containing about 200 litres, together with a 150 watt submersible pump delivering approximately 70 litres/minute to a head of 3 metres complete the system fixtures. A possible layout for the system is shown in fig 32 but the final arrangement will depend on the available space and the preference of the culturist, and as long as all the components are readily accessible it does not really matter.

All plumbing in the system should consist of plastic pipe and

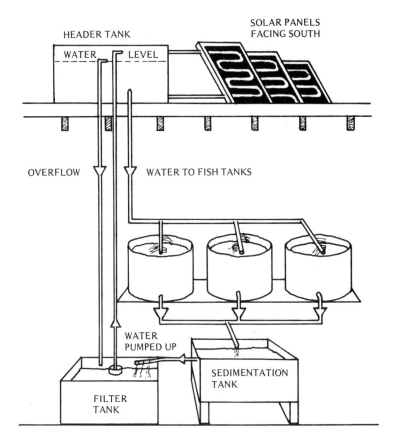

HEADER TANK

SOLAR PANELS
FACING SOUTH

WATER — LEVEL

OVERFLOW

WATER TO FISH TANKS

WATER
PUMPED UP

SEDIMENTATION
TANK

FILTER
TANK

Fig. 32 Components of a Recycling System

fittings of 20, 30 or 40mm internal diameter, as indicated, and some thought should be given to the layout which minimises the length of pipework involved.

Construction of the Fish Tanks
Any of the materials we have already described would be suitable, such as wood, glass fibre, welded polypropylene sheet etc, but one economical alternative would be to make them from old oil drums. Since these are generally smaller than our recommended tank sizes (about 75cm in diameter), more would be required to meet the volume requirement of 1 cubic metre — probably four in practice. They should of course be thoroughly cleaned, and preferably lined with glass fibre or a hard-wearing resin to render them non-toxic.

All the tanks should be supported on a strong framework, with their tops about 1.20 metres above the ground, the exact height depending on the most convenient working height for the culturist. Each should have a central drain pipe in 40mm pipe, about 50cm high, surrounded by an outer 75cm jacket in 50—55mm pipe. These jackets should have a cut-away at their bottoms to permit water evacuation from the tanks, the size of the cut-away depending on the size of the fish in the tanks — very small fish should have a jacket bottom of plastic netting.

The tanks should be supplied with water from 20mm pipe crossing the tank in the manner shown in the figure, and perforated so that parallel jets of water strike the water surface obliquely and impart a clockwise flow in the tanks. This aids the self-cleaning action of the tanks, and the jetting action of the water inflow improves oxygenation. Each tank inflow should be separately tapped to permit flow regulation and should be fed from a single downpipe from the header tank in 30mm pipe.

Construction of the Filter

The submerged filter consists of the filter medium supported on a perforated plate, with an under-gravel reservoir from which the pump draws its water, contained within an oblong tank. The tank may be made from marine plywood coated internally with a waterproof resin, and should rest on the floor because the weight of the filter medium is considerable. It should be about 2 metres long by 1 wide, and 50 to 60cm deep.

The filter medium itself can consist of a variety of materials, but the simplest to obtain is the mixed gravel used in concrete. This must be thoroughly washed free from sand before use, and it should consist of angular particles measuring between 4 and 15mm in diameter. Crushed oyster or cockle shells should be incorporated with this gravel

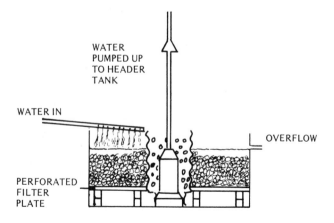

WATER PUMPED UP TO HEADER TANK

WATER IN

OVERFLOW

PERFORATED FILTER PLATE

Fig. 33 **Filter Tank**

on a 1:5 basis (i.e. 1 part of shells to 5 parts of gravel) to provide buffering capacity.

The medium should rest on a perforated plate which is supported about 15cm above the bottom of the tank. The plate should be drilled with holes just small enough to retain the gravel (about 4—5mm) and supported at regular intervals over its underside with bricks or wooden blocks. The plate can be made from corrugated or plain plastic sheet about 5—6mm thick, and should be sealed to the edges of the tank with a rubber or foam wedge.

The plate should also have a central hole through which the submersible pump is inserted, and this must be surrounded with drainpipe to prevent the gravel from caving in. It should support gravel to a depth of 25cm, and water should be maintained to a depth of about 8cm above the surface of the gravel by a suitably positioned overflow in the side of the filter tank.

The pump should discharge into the header tank via 30mm pipe, and the header tank should be fitted with a similar sized overflow which returns excess water to the filter. Although the total flow to the filter from the fish tanks should never exceed 60 litres/minute, the 70 litre flow of the pump is necessary to maintain the carrying capacity of the system. Water returned from the header tank to the filter without having passed through the fish tanks is important for supplying the oxygen needs of the filter and is not surplus to requirement.

The Header Tank

An ordinary domestic header tank would be quite suitable, and it would need to be fitted with three connections; an overflow 8—10cm below the top of the tank, returning water to the filter; an inlet from the pump slightly above the level of the overflow and an outlet to the fish tanks about 2—3cm above the bottom of the tank. All connections should be made in 30mm pipework.

The Sedimentation Tank

This could be made of marine plywood, and should have the same dimensions as the filter tank. It should also be supported some 10—15cm off the floor, to permit easy draining and provide a slight head for the outflow water to pass into the filter. The waste water from the fish tanks is introduced at one end of the sedimentation tank and passes to the filter at the other, having traversed a series of baffles on its way.

Inflow to the tank should be by way of 40mm piping, and this should discharge through a 'T' piece at the bottom of the tank, in front of a slanting bundle of pipes which run the whole length and width of the tank and are inclined toward the water surface at the outflow end of the sedimentation tank. These help to remove suspended solids by slowing down the water flow and distributing it throughout the whole tank volume, as well as providing a large surface area for trapping particles.

Outflow to the filter should also be through 40mm pipe, and it helps to improve oxygenation in the filter water if this outflow is delivered through a length of perforated pipe above the filter water surface.

The bundles of pipe in the sedimentation tank should be tied together (preferably with rotproof nylon cord) so that they can be removed complete for cleaning purposes. This should be done every week, or less depending on the accumulation of settled matter, while the accessible bottom of the sedimentation tank should be siphoned clear every day.

Water Inflow

The usual water make-up recommended for recycling systems is about 1–2% of the system volume per day. An inflow of fresh water is necessary both to make up for losses from evaporation and seepage (if the system has been built properly, there should not be any leaks!) and to keep the recycled water in good condition. It flushes out toxic products like nitrite, which need only accumulate to very low levels to have an effect on the fish, and prevents the water taking on the yellow-brown tinge that is characteristic of 'aged' aquarium water. However, a system should be capable of running for at least 2–3 weeks without any water make-up at all if it is functioning correctly and precautions are taken against evaporation.

The total volume of the system is about 1200 litres for the fish tanks, just under 1000 litres for the sedimentation tank, 200 litres for the header tank, plus the volume of the filter. We do not count the volume of the gravel in the water volume of the system, but it does contain some water, usually about 25% of its volume. The volume of the filter is thus approximately 600 litres and the total volume of the system is just a bit less than 3000 litres. An inflow of 1–2% of this is rather small, about 40ml/minute, and we would suggest an inflow of about a quarter of a litre per minute (250ml/minute) or 12% of the system volume per day, especially when keeping trout in the system. Lower inflows would be necessary when keeping the water warm, however, if the temperature difference between the system water and the incoming water is large. Make up water increases the carrying capacity of a system, and is useful as a safety factor in emergencies.

Preparing for Stocking

Before fish can be kept in a recycling system in any quantity, some time should be allowed for the filter to accumulate sufficient numbers of bacteria to cope with the normal pollutional loading. Preconditioning usually takes about three weeks to a month, and is effected by gradually increasing the stocking density to maximum. A few table sized fish should be bought and placed in the system some three weeks before proper stocking takes place, to get the filter established. They should be starved for one week, and then fed at an increasing rate for the following 10 days until they are eating as much food as they will take in four daily feeds. If anything should go wrong, and the fish appear unwell, the water make-up should be turned up. The advantage of stocking with a few large fish to begin with is that if any of them die, they can be eaten, whereas a loss of more sensitive fry would have to be written off completely.

Our suggested husbandry schedules do not bring the system up to its calculated carrying capacity until about 6 weeks after stocking; in this time the load is gradually increasing and should allow the filter time to adapt. It is still advisable to keep a close watch on the fish for the first three months, to try and detect any signs of stress or discomfort before they are manifested as fish deaths.

Management of Recycling Systems

Because the total weight of fish that can be kept in a recycling system is comparatively small, much stricter control over the growth of the fish, stocking and cropping is required if fish yield is to be on a continuous basis. It is necessary to maximise the growth of the fish as far as possible, and to accept that greater advance planning and adherence to management schedules is required than with pond farming. It is also necessary to accept fish of a slightly smaller size for eating at times than would be commercially acceptable.

In this recycling system, we have based our suggested management strategy on a superior food conversion than was allowed for the ponds, and a higher feeding rate, but all are readily attainable. The greater control exercised over fish in confined surroundings make feeding and general husbandry simpler, and we have assumed a food conversion of 1.5 for catfish and trout, and 1.6 for carp. Tilapia require a very different approach to husbandry, and it is more difficult to predict the food conversion. Food conversions of 1.1 are considered normal in commercial culture of trout, and we have demonstrated equally good food conversions in carp, so our working figures are by no means over-optimistic.

We would suggest that trout, catfish and carp are fed on pelleted diets, because these are easy to dispense, store and handle, as well as maintaining superior water quality in the system. Commercial rations are suitable, but in the next chapter we have outlined the formulation and manufacture of complete fish diets at home, and with a little practice and experimentation it should be possible to make diets more economically than they can be bought.

HUSBANDRY

KEEPING RAINBOW TROUT

The carrying capacity of a system containing rainbow trout at a water temperature of 16°C and being fed at 2% of their body weight per day is in the region of 21kg. Based on this carrying capacity, we have worked out a possible stocking schedule which allows the continuous cropping of up to 2.5kg of fish per week. The only real constraint is that four fish *must* be removed every week much of the time, which means that a few fish would have to be frozen if none were wanted during a particular week, or given away.

Apart from the carrying capacity of the system, the other factor which must be accounted for in any husbandry schedule is the seasonal availability of the fish. We have shown how to stock with two different sizes of trout, 5g and 70g, the larger of which is generally available from January to September each year. The smaller fish are usually available from January to June. Only one stocking per year is required with both sizes, so these can easily be fitted into times of availability.

The stocking schedule should be capable of producing edible fish of an individual weight of about 150g some 8 weeks after the system is commissioned. We have based the expected weekly weights on a feeding rate (initially) of 2% of the body weight, and a food conversion of 1.5. This means that the fish should grow at 1.3% of their body weight per day. Bear in mind that altering the amount of food fed on a weekly basis means that the fish are being fed at a lower percentage of their body weight at the end of the week than they were at the beginning. Small fluctuations in growth will probably even themselves out, but an average growth rate much lower than predicted merits investigation.

We have not listed the quantity of food to be given to the fish, but this can easily be calculated from the information given, and should in any case be based on the fish themselves.

Stocking

After preconditioning the filter, the system should be stocked with 150 fish of about 5g each, and 120 fish of about 70g. Only 140 of the smaller fish and 112 of the larger fish are needed for culinary purposes, the extra fish being allowed for mortalities. Mortalities in a recycling system should be low because of the close control over the fish, and we have allowed for 6% mortality as opposed to 10% in the ponds. If the extra fish have not died by the time they reach an edible size, then they should be culled. There is no need to allow for mortality when the fish are of an edible size, since any deaths can be eaten!

All these fish should be fed at 2% of their body weight per day, given in at least three portions, preferably more for the smaller fish. By week 8, the larger fish will have reached an edible size and cropping can commence. At the end of week 9, the feeding rate of the edible fish should be reduced to 1% per day, to keep the total weight of fish in the system below the carrying capacity and to reduce the cost of the food.

The smaller fish should be cropped at the beginning of week 36, as the larger fish are used up. Feeding should be reduced to 1% at the beginning of week 38, and the system reaches its maximum weight of fish during the following weeks. If problems develop because of over-stocking at this stage, a few more fish should be culled or feeding ceased for a while, particularly if temperatures rise above 15°C.

At the beginning of week 55, a fresh batch of 150 small fish should be placed in the system, and fed at 2% of their body weight per day. As the stock of edible fish is gradually reduced, the system should be restocked with 85, 70g fish as an interim measure while the smaller fish are growing to a suitable size. These should be cropped at the beginning of week 71, but the feeding rate is not reduced to 1% until week 77, to maintain the system at capacity, and provide larger fish for eating.

The younger fish are cropped from week 91 onwards, and the stocking of the system in future years is a repeat from week 38 to week 90.

From weeks 35–57, when the larger fish give the system its heaviest stocking density in weight terms, it would be a good idea to split the fish between two tanks. Always make maximum use of the installed facilities, and use all three tanks as much as possible. This provides some insurance — for example, if a waste pipe were to become blocked in one tank, then not all the fish would be lost (at the worst) if they were distributed between the three tanks. From weeks 63–70, all three tanks will be in use in any case, because three separate size ranges are stocked simultaneously.

General Maintenance

The filter surface should be cleaned weekly, the sedimentation tank daily and a brush should occasionally be passed down the outflows from the fish tanks. Manufacturer's instructions should be followed diligently with regard to pump maintenance, particularly lubrication if this is periodically required.

Sometimes the top layers of the filter can become clogged and the gravel should be dug over to a depth of a few cm, the murky water being flushed out through the overflow before the water supply to the rest of the system is restored.

Problems of disease can largely be circumvented by following the quarantine schedule described in chapter 10 for each new batch of fish, but should disease be introduced into a system at any time, treatment is simplified by the small water volume and control over the fish. Unfortunately, most of the treatments effective against disease organisms are very effective against the bacteria in the filter as well, and post-

Table 11 Stocking and Management Schedules for Rainbow Trout

Week No.	TANK 1		TANK 2		TANK 3		Total System Weight (kg)
	Individual Weight (g)	Total Weight (kg)	Individual Weight (g)	Total Weight (kg)	Individual Weight (g)	Total Weight (kg)	
0	5.00	0.75 *120 fish*	70	8.40 *140 fish*	—	—	9.15
1	5.47	0.82	76.62	9.19	—	—	10.01
2	5.99	0.90	83.87	10.06	—	—	10.96
3	6.56	0.98	91.81	11.02	—	—	12.00
4	7.18	1.08	100.50	12.06	—	—	13.14
5	7.86	1.18	110.01	13.20	—	—	14.38
6	8.60	1.29	120.42	14.45	—	—	15.74
7	9.42	1.41	131.81	15.82 *reduce to 112 fish*	—	—	17.23
8	10.31	1.55	144.28	15.58 *start cropping*	—	—	17.13
9	11.28	1.69	150.97	15.70 *reduce feeding to 1%*	—	—	17.39
10	12.35	1.85	157.98	15.80	—	—	17.65
11	13.52	2.03	165.31	15.87	—	—	17.90
12	14.80	2.22	172.98	15.91	—	—	18.13
13	16.20	2.43	181.00	15.93	—	—	18.36
14	17.73	2.66	189.40	15.91	—	—	18.57
15	19.41	2.91	198.19	15.86	—	—	18.77
16	21.24	3.19	207.38	15.76	—	—	18.95
17	23.25	3.49	217.01	15.62	—	—	19.11
18	25.45	3.82	227.08	15.44	—	—	19.26
19	27.86	4.18	237.61	15.21	—	—	19.39

No.							
20	30.50	4.58	248.63	14.92	—	—	19.49
21	33.39	5.01	260.17	14.57	—	—	19.57
22	36.54	5.48	272.24	14.16	—	—	19.64
23	40.00	6.00	284.87	13.67	—	—	19.67
24	43.78	6.57	298.09	13.12	—	—	19.68
25	47.93	7.20	311.92	12.48	—	—	19.67
26	52.47	7.87	326.39	11.75	—	—	19.62
27	57.43	8.61	341.54	10.93	—	—	19.54
28	62.87	9.43	357.38	10.01	—	—	19.44
29	68.82	10.37	373.96	8.98	—	—	19.35
30	75.33	11.30	391.32	7.83	—	—	19.13
31	82.46	12.37	409.47	6.55	—	—	18.92
32	90.26	13.54	428.46	5.14	—	—	18.68
33	98.80	14.82	448.35	3.59	—	—	18.41
34	108.15	16.22	469.15	1.88	—	—	18.10
35	119.92	16.79	490.92	—	—	—	16.79
36	131.27	17.85 *start cropping*	—	—	—	—	17.85
37	143.69	18.97	—	—	—	—	18.97
38	150.35	19.25 *reduce feeding to 1%*	—	—	—	—	19.25
39	157.33	19.51	—	—	—	—	19.51
40	164.63	19.75	—	—	—	—	19.75
41	172.27	19.98	—	—	—	—	19.98
42	180.26	20.19	—	—	—	—	20.19
43	188.62	20.37	—	—	—	—	20.37
44	197.38	20.53	—	—	—	—	20.53
45	206.54	20.65	—	—	—	—	20.65
46	216.12	20.75	—	—	—	—	20.75
47	226.14	20.81	—	—	—	—	20.81
48	236.64	20.83	—	—	—	—	20.83
49	247.62	20.80	—	—	—	—	20.80
50	259.11	20.73	—	—	—	—	20.73

reduce to 140 fish (row 35)

Week No.	Individual Weight (g)	Total Weight (kg)	Individual Weight (g)	Total Weight (kg)	Individual Weight (g)	Total Weight (kg)	Total System Weight (kg)
51	271.13	20.61	—	—	—	—	20.61
52	283.71	20.42	—	—	—	—	20.42
53	296.87	20.19	—	—	—	—	20.19
54	310.64	19.88	—	— *restock 150 fish*	—	—	19.88
55	325.06	19.50	5.00	0.75	—	—	20.25
56	340.14	19.05	5.47	0.82	—	—	19.87
57	355.92	18.51	5.99	0.90	—	—	19.41
58	372.43	17.88	6.56	0.98	—	—	18.86
59	389.71	17.15	7.18	1.08	—	—	18.23
60	407.80	16.31	7.86	1.18	—	—	17.49
61	426.72	15.36	8.60	1.29	—	—	16.65
62	446.52	14.29	9.42	1.41	—	—	15.70
63	467.23	13.08	10.31	1.55	70	5.95 *restock 85 fish*	20.63
64	488.91	11.73	11.28	1.69	76.62	6.51	19.94
65	511.59	10.23	12.35	1.85	83.87	7.13	19.21
66	535.33	8.57	13.52	2.03	91.81	7.80	18.39
67	560.17	5.76	14.80	2.22	100.50	8.54	17.48
68	586.16	4.69	16.20	2.43	110.01	9.35	16.47
69	613.35	2.45	17.73	2.66	120.42	10.24 *reduce to 80 fish*	15.35
70	641.81	—	19.41	2.91	131.81	11.20 *start cropping*	14.11
71	—	—	21.24	3.19	144.28	10.97	14.15
72	—	—	23.25	3.49	157.93	11.37	14.86
73	—	—	25.45	3.82	172.88	11.76	15.58
74	—	—	27.86	4.18	189.25	12.11	16.29

75	—	—	30.50	4.58	207.15	12.43	17.01
76	—	—	33.39	5.01	226.75	12.70 *reduce feeding to 1%*	17.71
77	—	—	36.54	5.48	248.21	12.90	18.39
78	—	—	40.00	6.00	259.72	12.47	18.47
79	—	—	43.78	6.57	271.78	11.95	18.53
80	—	—	47.93	7.20	284.38	11.38	18.57
81	—	—	52.47	7.87	297.58	10.71	18.58
82	—	—	57.43	8.61	311.39	9.96	18.57
83	—	—	62.87	9.43	325.83	9.12	18.55
84	—	—	68.82	10.37	340.95	8.18	18.55
85	—	—	75.33	11.30	356.77	7.14	18.41
86	—	—	82.46	12.37	373.32	5.97	18.34
87	—	—	90.26	13.54	390.64	4.69	18.23
88	—	—	98.80	14.82	408.77	3.27	18.09
89	—	—	108.15	16.22	427.74	1.71	17.93
90	—	—	119.92	16.79 *reduce to 140 fish*	447.56	—	16.79
91	—	—	131.27	17.85 *start cropping*	—	—	17.85
92	—	—	143.69	18.97	—	—	18.97
93	—	—	150.35	19.25 *reduce feeding to 1%*	—	—	19.25
94	—	—	157.33	19.51	—	—	19.51
95	—	—	164.63	19.75	—	—	19.75
96	—	—	172.27	19.98	—	—	19.98
97	—	—	180.26	20.19	—	—	20.19
98	—	—	188.62	20.37	—	—	20.37
99	—	—	197.38	20.53	—	—	20.53
100	—	—	206.54	20.65	—	—	20.65

treatment recovery of the filter as well as the fish is usually needed. This means turning up the water inflow and possibly providing extra oxygenation for the fish tanks via an aquarium air pump until nitrifying capacity is re-established.

Other Considerations

One drawback to the keeping of rainbow trout in such a recycling system is the cost. If they are fed on commercial rations, the costs of these together with the cost of electricity for pumping and the outlay for the fish themselves puts a cost on the fish produced equivalent to their current wholesale price, with no payback for the investment in the system. However, if home-made diets are used, costs are reduced somewhat and work out at about 5—10% below market prices; the payback on the system is then about 2% per year.

Systems containing carp are more competitive, but catfish work out about the same as trout. Since tilapia don't have a stable market price in Europe and the USA at the moment, it is difficult to work out the economics of their culture, but at favourable prices, it is somewhat similar to that of carp. Systems smaller than the one we have described are uneconomic to run, while increasing the output reduces the overall costs. Costs of the fish themselves can be reduced by producing ones own eggs, but this requires an extra investment in hatching and rearing equipment — plus time! Keeping fish for eating in a recycling system is thus more of a hobby on the scale we have described, because including time and labour costs in an economic appraisal confers a higher price on all the fish than their current wholesale price.

Using alternative sources of energy like the wind and the sun for pumping and heating reduces the running costs of a system, but increases the initial outlay, which would probably not be regained within the lifetime of the system. Intensive production of fish in a recycling system is therefore most suited to a co-operative venture on a slightly larger scale — especially when one considers that the output from our system is probably too much for a single family. We have described design considerations and operating schedules which can easily be adapted to a larger enterprise, and it is up the individual to decide on the scale and the merits of recycling systems versus ponds. Where space is available and water supply little problem, ponds have a considerable cost advantage over recycling systems together with a lower maintenance requirement and daily work input.

KEEPING MIRROR CARP

Having denigrated our system, we will now go on to describe its use for the other species. Carp, catfish and tilapia are all warm water species, and to achieve a satisfactory growth rate all the year round it is necessary to warm the water artificially. To keep heating costs to an acceptable minimum, we would suggest the incorporation of solar panels into the system, with a back-up heat source for the winter months. This back-up could be an electric immersion heater, or better still a heat-exchange circuit with a gas or oil-fired heater. Homes with central heating could, with a little ingenuity, use this as a source of heat for the system — with the option of putting something back from the solar panels during the summer.

Efficient insulation is important, and the stability offered by a large thermal mass — the water in the system — means the water temperature rises and falls slowly. All the tanks should be wrapped with a single layer of shiny aluminium foil followed by at least 3cm of polystyrene or foam rubber insulation. The polystyrene sheet sold as insulating wall paper could be useful here. All the tanks should be fitted with lids to reduce evaporative heat loss, although the lids on the fish tanks should let a little light filter through. A thermostat should be included somewhere to prevent temperatures rising too much during the summer.

A solar collector of 2 square metres in surface area would be adequate to meet the heating requirements of the system, because the water temperatures involved are much lower than those preferred for domestic use. Although the water supply to the panels could be obtained from a small diameter take-off from the output side of the pump, regulation would then have to be by hand or solenoid valve, and it is therefore easier to provide a separate small pump for the solar circuit. Inflow to and outflow from the panel could lead into the header tank, reducing the length of pipework required if the panels are situated on the roof of the building.

Operating Temperature

The optimum temperature for the growth of carp is about 28°C, but in practice only a small increase in the rate of growth is realised above 24°C. It is thus not worth maintaining the system above this temperature — it is a waste of energy. At higher temperatures, the carrying capacity is also decreased, and we have allowed for a maximum temperature in the system of 30°C.

At our proposed feeding rate of 4% of the body weight per day and at a temperature of 30°C, the oxygen demand of the system for carp is 920mg of oxygen/kg of fish/hour. The rate of supply of usable oxygen from 85% saturated water at this temperature is 14700mg per hour, and the carrying capacity is thus (14700/920) or about 16kg of fish. At 24°C, the carrying capacity is increased to approximately 19kgs.

In our suggested stocking schedule, the fish are only fed at 4% of their body weight at the lower total system weights. Once they have reached an edible size, feeding is reduced to 1%, so that maximum weights in the system correspond to periods of minimum feeding, and the carrying capacity is never exceeded.

Table 12 Stocking and Management Schedule for Mirror Carp

Week No.	Individual Weight (g)		Total Weight (kg)	Individual Weight (g)		Total Weight (kg)		Total System Weight (kg)
0	5.00	stock 55 fish	0.28	100	stock 36 fish	3.60		3.88
1	5.94		0.33	118.87		4.28		4.61
2	7.06		0.39	141.30		5.09		5.48
3	8.40		0.46	167.96		6.05		6.51
4	9.98		0.55	199.65		7.19		7.74
5	11.87		0.65	237.32		8.54		9.19
6	14.10		0.78	282.10		10.16		10.94
7	16.77		0.92	335.33	reduce to 34 fish	12.07		13.00
8	19.93		1.10	398.60	start cropping	12.76	reduce to 1%	13.86
9	23.69		1.30	416.37		12.49		13.79
10	28.16		1.55	434.93		12.18		13.73
11	33.47		1.84	454.32		11.81		13.65
12	39.79		2.19	474.57		11.39		13.58
13	47.30		2.60	495.73		10.91		13.51
14	56.22		3.09	517.83		10.36		13.45
15	66.83		3.68	540.91		9.74		13.42
16	79.44		4.37	565.02		9.04		13.41
17	94.43		5.19	590.21		8.26		13.45
18	112.25		6.17	616.52		7.40		13.57
19	133.43		7.34	644.01		6.44		13.78
20	158.60		8.72	672.71		5.38		14.10
21	188.53		10.37	702.70		4.22		14.59
22	224.10		12.33	734.03		2.94		15.27

23	266.38	14.65	766.75	1.53	16.18
24	316.64 *reduce to 50 fish*	17.42	800.93	—	17.42
25	376.39 *start cropping*	18.06	5.00 *restock 55 fish*	0.28	18.34
26	393.17 *reduce to 1%*	18.09	5.94	0.33	18.42
27	410.69	18.07	7.06	0.39	18.46
28	429.00	18.02	8.40	0.46	18.48
29	448.13	17.93	9.98	0.55	18.48
30	468.10	17.79	11.87	0.65	18.44
31	488.97	17.60	14.10	0.78	18.38
32	510.77	17.37	16.77	0.92	18.29
33	533.54	17.07	19.93	1.10	18.17
34	557.32	16.72	23.69	1.30	18.02
35	582.17	16.30	28.16	1.55	17.85
36	608.12	15.81	33.47	1.84	17.65
37	635.23	15.25	39.79	2.19	17.44
38	663.55	14.60	47.30	2.60	17.20
39	693.13	13.86	56.22	3.09	16.95
40	724.03	13.03	66.83	3.68	16.71
41	756.30	12.10	79.44	4.37	16.47
42	790.00	11.06	94.43	5.19	16.25
43	825.24	9.90	112.25	6.17	16.07
44	862.03	8.62	133.43	7.34	15.96
45	900.45	7.20	158.60	8.72	15.92
46	940.59	5.64	188.53	10.37	16.01
47	982.53	3.93	224.10	12.33	16.26
48	1026.33	2.05	266.38	14.65	16.70
49	1072.68	—	316.64 *reduce to 50 fish*	17.42	17.42
50	5.00 *restock 55 fish*	0.28	376.30 *start cropping*	18.06 *reduce to 1%*	18.34

Stocking

The increased edible weight of carp compared with trout means that the same number of fish cannot be cropped from the recycling system as from the ponds. As we mentioned in connection with the pond farming of carp, 100kg of carp per year is probably more than one family could comfortably eat, so our stocking schedule seeks to produce half this number of fish i.e. two edible fish per week.

A problem that may be encountered concerns the availability of fingerling carp. After the first twelve months, as the system comes into continuous operation, it is stocked twice a year with about 50 small carp. Some inquiries should be made of nearby suppliers as to the availability of carp of this size throughout the year. If, as is commonly the case, fish are only available during the autumn and following spring, then a year's supply will have to be purchased at one time. Half the fish should then be kept in a separate facility at as low a temperature as possible and at a low feeding rate (approximately maintenance ration) until they are ready to be grown on in the recycling system. Although buying in bulk may secure a slightly lower initial price for the fish, this is more than lost by the cost of the food needed to hold them for six months, and it is preferable to buy in fish as they are needed.

At higher temperatures, preconditioning of the filter should not take as long, and once this is achieved the system should be stocked initially with about 55 small (5g) carp and about 36 larger (100g) ones. Both lots of fish are fed at 4% of their body weight to begin with, and this is reduced to 1% for the larger fish in week 8 when some will have reaced an edible size. Always crop the largest fish first. By week 7, only the intended number of fish (34) should be left, and cropping can begin in week 8 (see table 12).

Two fish per week are then taken until week 25, when the fingerlings reach an edible size and may be culled. Only 50 fish should be left by this time, and the system should be simultaneously restocked with another 55 small fish as cropping of the first batch commences. The feeding rate of the edible fish should now be reduced to 1% at the beginning of week 26, while the new arrivals are fed at 4% of their body weight. By week 50, these are ready for eating, and the system should be restocked with another 55 fingerlings, and so on.

KEEPING CATFISH AND TILAPIA

The carrying capacity of the system for catfish at 30°C and fed 3% of their body weight is about 8kg. Their high oxygen requirement and the need for warm water render them less suitable for farming in recycling systems than either of the preceding two species, and an efficient oxygenating facility such as a venturi would have to be incorporated in the system to offset this. With water at 100% saturation, the carrying capacity at 30°C is increased to about 14kg. Fed at 3% of their body weight, growth would be adequate, but more frequent restockings are required to compensate for the reduced carrying capacity.

We have not included a stocking schedule for catfish because their culture is so similar to carp, and following the preceding examples the culturist should be able to work out his own management strategy. Fingerling catfish are available for most of the year from suppliers within the USA, which simplifies the problem of frequent restocking.

The carrying capacity for tilapia is the same as that for carp, about 19kg at 24°C and a feeding rate of 4%. However, since the fish are liable to reproduce in the system, we cannot forecast the total weight with any accuracy and management is a haphazard affair.

Reproduction is desirable because tilapia cannot be bought at regular intervals in the same way as the other species, so to keep production going, recruitment must also be continuous. Exerting some measure of control over the reproduction, which is essential, requires several modifications of the system. Parents are less likely to reproduce in circular tanks and even if they do, the young are likely to be washed out with the outflow unless very fine gauze is placed over the outer jacket. This will interfere with the removal of faeces from the larger fish and it is in any case useful that fry should be removed from the system in this way, to be managed separately.

One tank should be specially modified for rearing the fry. It should be rectangular and drained from the bottom centre. The whole floor of the tank could be covered with gauze, fine enough to retain the smallest fry, and divided into three or four compartments by transverse gauze screens. The tank itself should be about 1 metre long, 50—60cm wide and 30—40cm deep. The level of water in the tank is controlled by a swivel pipe which discharges into the sedimentation tank.

Spawning pairs can be placed in one compartment, and kept there until the female is incubating the fertilised eggs in her mouth. The male should be removed and returned to the other tanks. Once the fry are venturing from the female's mouth, she should be removed and the young placed in the next compartment. They should be fed on fine pelleted food until they reach a large enough size to be transferred to the main tanks, progressing through the compartments in the rearing tank as they grow.

Only a half-dozen pairs of tilapia should be placed in the system to begin with, in order to build up stocks of young tilapia. As the total weight of fish in the system cannot be predicted, it is important to familiarise oneself with the behaviour of the fish and the system for a period of time before beginning to crop. After a while, it will be possible to judge how close to the carrying capacity one has got and when fish need culling. It would probably be twelve months before any sustainable yield could be achieved.

Feeding of the tilapia is best done with pellets. These could be made at home and based on plant materials, with a small amount of animal material to balance the diet. Much of our advice about feeding in ponds applies to recycling systems as well.

Fish should be cropped at the size and discretion of the culturist, as it is impossible to make any predictions of the likely yield. Growth rate will be rapid and males will usually be the first to be cropped because of their faster growth, but tilapia culture in recycling systems and small ponds remains very much a pioneering field.

FOOD PRESENTATION

The manner in which food is presented for the fish to eat has an important bearing on how efficiently they utilise it for growth. The frequency of feeding is dependent on the size and species of fish, as well as water temperature, water quality and daylength.

For all species, fry (or fish less than 4cm long) require feeding more often than larger fish. In intensive rearing, fry really need feeding at hourly intervals throughout the day, especially when they are of the warm water species.

From fingerling to table size, rainbow trout do not need to be presented with food more than two or three times a day, allowing as much time to elapse between feeds as possible. They will still take food more often given the opportunity, but over the whole day will only consume as much as they can in three feeds. Catfish follow the same pattern, while carp and tilapia are 'nibblers', eating small amounts of food almost continually throughout the day. Hand feeding makes

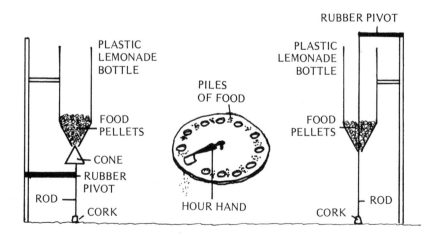

Fig. 34 **Automatic Feeders**

this impractical, so a minimum of three feeds per day would have to suffice.

When hand feeding to a set percentage of the body weight, food should be distributed a little at a time, giving the fish chance to eat it all before giving any more. Cease feeding as soon as the majority of the fish are disinterested in the food, not when there are no fish left feeding. This prevents any wastage. Least effort is involved when a set ration is distributed by an automatic feeder of some sort, probably the best way of feeding carp and tilapia (fig 34). Demand feeders, as they are commonly called, are particularly useful in ponds where it is difficult to judge when the fish have finished feeding if the water is slightly murky. Hand feeding in recycling systems has the advantage of close observation of the feeding response of the fish, which is always a good indicator of their well-being.

8 fish nutrition

In all fish farms, the cost of supplemental food is the greatest recurring cost and it is in the interest of the farmer to get a good return on this investment in terms of fish weight gain. The extent to which a food is utilised by fish is influenced by many factors, such as the environment, the presence of disease and the age and genetic constitution of the farmed fish species. However, the most basic factor is the composition of the food and how closely it matches the fish's nutritional requirement.

All animals need certain ingredients in their diet, these being proteins, fats, carbohydrates, vitamins and minerals. The required quantity and quality of each of these dietary constituents varies from species to species, and to a lesser extent within each species. The nutritional requirements of fish are not completely understood, but a broad knowledge of the function of each of the constituents mentioned above will help in the choice of the most suitable commercial ration for the fish or in formulating diets.

Dietary Protein

Since the flesh of fish is composed predominantly of protein, and without it fish cannot grow, protein is an important major constituent of a fish diet. Both the quantity and quality of the dietary protein must be correct in relation to the requirements of the fish species being cultured.

Different proteins are composed of various combinations of smaller units known as amino acids. When a food is ingested, the protein content is broken down during digestion and the constituent amino acids absorbed. These are then rebuilt into the body protein of the fish, leading to growth. There are approximately twenty-five different amino acids commonly found in natural proteins and proteins from different sources contain differing proportions of these.

Some of these amino acids are not essential dietary components because fish can synthesize them from other amino acids or nutrients. However, ten kinds of amino acids cannot be made either in sufficient quantities or at all by fish and must be present in the dietary protein. These are known as the essential amino acids. If they are not available from the food source, then body protein construction comes to a halt. This situation can be likened to a factory production line where an article is being made from bought-in components. If one of the key components is missing, the production line comes to a halt.

Table 13 The Essential Amino Acid Requirement of Salmonids and the Content of Two Common Protein Sources.

Essential Amino Acid Requirement of salmonids (% of dietary protein)		Essential Amino Acid Profile of a Fishmeal (% of protein)	Essential Amino Acid Profile of a Soyabean Meal (% of protein)
Arginine	6.0	5.6	7.5
Histidine	1.8	2.6	2.5
Isoleucine	2.2	4.4	4.7
Leucine	3.9	7.4	7.7
Lysine	5.0	7.3	6.2
Methionine (+Cystine)	4.0	3.9	2.5
Phenylalanine (+Tyrosine)	5.1	7.2	8.6
Threonine	2.2	4.9	4.3
Tryptophan	0.5	1.3	1.3
Valine	3.2	5.3	4.8

If one or several of the essential amino acids are present in less than the required quantity, then only some of the dietary protein can be used for growth and the rest must be 'burned' for energy.

As the protein content of a diet tends to be the most expensive ingredient, it is rather wasteful if it is used for energy rather than growth, so it pays to ensure that the essential amino acid balance of the dietary protein is as close to the known requirements as possible. Table 13 shows the essential amino acid requirements of salmonids, the only species for which they are accurately known, and the amount supplied by two common protein sources, fish meal and soyabean meal.

It can be seen that a diet containing only soyabean meal as the protein source would be deficient in methionine and cystine, which would restrict growth. Fish meal, on the other hand, contains nearly all the essential amino acids in the required quantities, the exception being arginine. The very high cost of fish meal unfortunately precludes its exclusive use in diets, and it is normally diluted with less expensive protein sources like soyabean meal and other plant proteins. A mixture of proteins would not have such an ideal amino acid profile, but would be effective and cheaper to manufacture.

The quality of the protein source is not the only consideration, as the gross protein requirements (the proportion of the diet containing protein necessary for optimal growth) must also be taken into account. In comparison with other farmed animals, the protein requirements of fish are rather high, but they make up for this by being better at converting their food into flesh. The gross protein requirement varies to some extent with the protein quality, the energy level of the diet, the digestibility of the protein, the size and species of fish and the water temperature and quality. With trout, the youngest fish need about 55% of their diet to be in the form of protein, but this falls off with age and the size of fish suggested would need 35—40% protein in their diet. Carp and channel catfish seem to follow the same sort of pattern, with the youngest fish having the highest gross protein requirements. Fingerling carp diets should contain about 38% protein for good growth at their optimal temperature, while catfish seem to need 30—36% at the same age.

Although water temperature and dietary energy level affect the gross protein requirements, in a practical sense it is too difficult and expensive to formulate diets for a variety of water temperatures, and some sort of compromise must be struck. In a diet for the fish, a balanced protein source included at 35—40% of the diet would be adequate for most fish species and environmental conditions.

One further consideration concerns the digestibility of a protein source. Vegetable proteins like soyabean have been found to be less digestible in trout than proteins of animal origin, because the digestive enzymes are unable to break down the vegetable cell walls and thus release the proteins inside. More omnivorous species like carp and tilapia are able to digest these cell walls and can utilise vegetable protein sources more effectively than trout, so a greater proportion may be included in their diet. Once digested, however, there would appear to be little difference in the extent to which plant proteins are retained for growth among species.

Dietary Lipids (Fats)

These substances have two roles in fish nutrition. Firstly they are the main energy yielding ingredients, especially for the more carnivorous species, and secondly they perform a major structural role as components of the body cell walls.

The term lipid covers many kinds of substances, ranging from simple fats and phospholipids based on the glycerol molecule, to non-glycerol based waxes and steroids. Of most concern here are the simple fats, which consist of various fatty acids linked to molecules of glycerol. The fatty acids themselves can be divided into two groups depending on whether they are saturated or unsaturated. The degree of unsaturation in a fat affects its melting point; fats with a high degree of polyunsaturation are liquids at normal temperatures, and are called oils.

The degree of unsaturation has an important bearing on the usefulness of a fat to a fish. Due to the construction of their digestive systems and the fact that they are 'cold-blooded', fish are not readily able to use fats which are solid at the temperatures of their surroundings, and thus need a supply of unsaturated fatty acids in their food. These can be supplied from sources such as soyabean, corn and fish oils.

Essential Fatty Acids

A certain group of unsaturated fatty acids are even more important in fish nutrition, and these are called the essential fatty acids. Analogous to the essential amino acids, they cannot be synthesised by fish from other fatty acids, and certain minimum levels must be supplied in the diet.

The EFA's belong to a group of fatty acids called the linolenic series and for trout, the requirement is around 1% of the diet. The vegetable oils (other than linseed) contain only very low levels of the linolenic fatty acids, and diets containing these as the only lipid source would soon cause dietary disease symptoms to occur. The best sources of the linolenic fatty acids are fish oils (herring, cod, menhaden salmon etc.) which contain 20–30%. Thus fish diets should contain at least 5% fish oil in order to meet the 1% dietary requirement for EFA's. Once this need is satisfied, it is theoretically possible to make up the rest of the lipid component of the diet with vegetable oils, but we would recommend a maximum of 3–4% vegetable oil in the diet. Carp have been shown to require about 1% of linoleic fatty acid in their diet, as well as 1% linolenic, and so should be supplied with a small percentage of vegetable oils.

The overall dietary level of fat is important as it can govern the extent to which the protein portion of the diet can be used for growth. If the fat level is too low, then some of the protein will be used to make up the energy deficit in the diet and the full potential of the diet for growth will not be realised. On the other hand, too high a fat level produces fatty fish which may be both unpalatable to the consumer and suffer from liver damage. Commercial trout rations vary in their fat content, but rarely contain much more than 15%, the average content being about 8%. For catfish diets, 8% is also normal. Commercial trout diets designed to maintain edible sized fish at market weight for short periods, and which are often fed to carp because of their lower cost, contain as little as 5% lipid. This would appear to be sub-optimal, if not actually deficient for carp, which again require about 8% lipid in their diets. Since tilapia appear to grow extremely well on diets suited

119

to carp, their requirements are probably similar, and should be assumed to be so in the absence of information to the contrary.

Dietary Carbohydrate

Together with fats, carbohydrates are the main energy providing nutrients of the diet, but no carbohydrates are essential and their absence does not provoke any ill effects. However, they are a cheaper energy source than lipid and as such are useful ingredients.

Carbohydrates range in their degree of complexity from very small molecules such as glucose to large polymers like celluloses and starches. The small unit sugars like glucose are reasonably well digested and absorbed by all fish — trout can assimilate over 90% of ingested sucrose or glucose. With the larger polymers, the situation is more complicated, there being considerable variation between species. A very common carbohydrate, starch, is poorly digested by trout (around 40%), but very well digested by carp. The extent of assimilation must be considered when deciding on the amount of carbohydrate to include in the diet.

Carnivorous species are not well adapted to metabolising large amounts of carbohydrate because of the low content in their natural diet. In consequence, their bodies are overwhelmed by carbohydrate-rich foods, and what cannot be used immediately for energy or stored in the form of glycogen remains in the blood. This causes a situation rather similar to that found in diabetic humans and can lead to the death of the fish. For trout, the less digestible the carbohydrate, the more it can be tolerated, but this is not the case with more omnivorous fish like carp, which can both digest and metabolise carbohydrate more efficiently.

Opinions vary on the allowable proportion of digestible carbohydrate in fish rations, but the concensus for trout and catfish is around 20%, which is equivalent to about 30–35% total carbohydrate in the diet. Data for carp and tilapia is more limited, but levels in the region of 30% digestible carbohydrate (40–50% total) may not be excessive.

Indigestible (fibrous) carbohydrates such as cellulose and hemicellulose, while not being of much nutritive value, probably do have a role in controlling the passage of food through the gut, as they do in humans. Manufactured feeds have a fibre (roughage) content of between 2 and 5%, which seems to cause no harm, but levels should not greatly exceed 5%.

Vitamins

Vitamins are defined as organic compounds which are required in small amounts for normal growth and maintenance of living organisms. Both mammals and fish appear to have similar qualitative vitamin requirements, but because certain metabolic processes are more important in

Table 14 Recommended Dietary Intake of Vitamins for Trout, Catfish and Carp

Vitamin	Function in the Body & Best Source	Recommended Dietary Intake (mg/kg of dry diet)		
		Trout 2000 IU*	*Catfish* 5,500 IU	*Carp* 4000–20,000 IU
Fat Soluble				
Vit. A	Vision, mucous secretion (Fish Oils, Liver)	2000 IU*	5,500 IU	4000–20,000 IU
Vit. D	Calcium & phosphorous metabolism (Fish Oils)	Not shown to be essential	Not shown to be essential	Not shown to be essential
Vit. E	Biological Anti-oxidant (Cereal Grains)	30mg	50mg	100mg
Vit. K	Blood Clotting (Fishmeal, Soya and Liver)	80mg	10mg	—
Water Soluble				
Thiamine (Vit. B1)	Enzymic Reactions (Yeasts, Cereal Grains, Fresh Meats)	10mg	20mg	Very small requirement unless diet rich in carbohydrate.
Riboflavin (Vit. B2)	Carbohydrate Metabolism (Yeasts, Cereal Grains, Oil Seeds)	20mg	20mg	7–10mg
Pyridoxine (Vit. B6)	Protein Metabolism (Yeasts, Cereal Grains)	10mg	20mg	About 5–6mg
Nicotinic Acid (Niacin)	Biochemical Carrier (Yeasts and most Protein)	150mg	100mg	28mg
Pantothenic Acid	Biochemical Carrier (Yeasts & Cereal Grains)	40mg	40mg	30–40mg
Inositol	Cell membrane formation (Yeasts, Liver, Cereals)	400mg	—	440mg
Biotin	Fatty acid metabolism (Yeasts, Liver)	1mg	1mg	1.5mg
Folic Acid	Biochemical Carrier (Yeasts, Cereal Grains)	5mg	5mg	Not essential
Choline	Cell membranes, nervous transmission (Pulses, Cereals, Protein)	3000 IU	—	—
Cyanocobalamin (Vit. B12)	Protein metabolism, blood formation (Yeasts, Liver)	0.02mg	0.02mg	Not essential
Ascorbic Acid (Vit. C)	Collagen synthesis, wound repair (Citrus Pulp)	100–150	30–50	30–50

3333 International Units (IU) of Vit. A are equal to 1mg of the pure vitamin.

121

fish than in mammals (and vice versa), quantitative requirements do vary slightly. To simplify matters, the table summarises the vitamin requirements of fish as they are understood, their function in the body and their recommended dietary levels and they are divided into two main groups, water and fat soluble.

Commercial foods contain a vitamin premix added before processing. These premixes contain most or all of the required vitamins to ensure adequate dietary levels, and the home formulator should have little difficulty in obtaining one from a feed manufacturer. Premixes are employed in most animal feeds and, provided the levels of each vitamin are known, and compare closely with the levels shown in the table, it is not absolutely vital to use a premix specifically formulated for fish. Despite evidence of some differences in vitamin requirements between fish species, a premix designed for trout or salmon should be suitable for carp, catfish and tilapia.

Minerals

For most animals at least 16 elements have been shown to be required for health and growth and the number may be closer to 25. Their roles in the body range from structural, as in bones, to the maintenance of ionic balance. For most terrestrial farm animals some knowledge of requirements is available, but virtually none is available for fish. Because of their capability of absorbing mineral elements directly from the surrounding water, the dietary requirement will vary to some degree with the concentration of an element in the water. The hardness of the water will therefore play a part in mineral nutrition, as hard water will contain many more dissolved minerals than soft. It has to be assumed that the overall mineral requirements of fish are not vastly dissimilar to those of land animals.

The table of elements is only meant as a rough guide for reference purposes, because many ingredients will contain a little of each element, and a compounded diet may contain adequate levels of all minerals. There is always a possibility, however, that the elements required in the largest amounts may be present in limiting quantities, which is a frequent occurrence with phosphorous. It would be prudent to add a little phosphorous in the form of di-calcium phosphate to bring the total dietary level to about 1%, especially if the water is very soft.

The commercial vitamin premixes also commonly contain several trace elements, which would ensure that none of these were missing from the diet. Care must be taken to avoid adding too many minerals to the diet, for several are toxic at concentrations only slightly above their required levels. Commercial rations rarely contain more than 9–11% of minerals (as ash), and it would be wise to limit ash to 10% of the diet.

Table 15 The Mineral Requirements of Fish

Element	Function in the Body	Dietary Sources
Calcium	Skeleton, nervous transmission blood coagulation, muscle contraction, tissue fluids.	Water, Fishmeal, meat and bone meal.
Phosphorous	Skeleton, phospholipids of cell membranes, nucleic acids, general metabolism	Fishmeal, meat and bone meal.
Potassium	Osmotic regulation of body fluids; nerve and muscle action	Plant materials
Sodium	Osmotic regulation, acid-base balance	Animal materials
Chlorine	Osmotic regulation, acid-base balance, gastric secretion	Fish and meat meals
Sulphur	Not required as free sulphur but as the sulphur amino acids (methionine and cystine)	Fish and meat meals

TRACE ELEMENTS

Element	Function in the Body	Dietary Sources
Magnesium	Bone formation, enzymic reactions	Fishmeal, yeast, wheat bran
Iron	Blood formation	Blood meal, most feed ingredients
Copper	Blood formation, enzymic reactions	Most feeding ingredients
Iodine	Component of hormones	Fish meal, seaweed meal
Cobalt	Component of Vit. B12 Enzymic reactions	Most feed ingredients
Manganese	Enzymic reactions	Rice bran, wheat.
Zinc	Enzymic reactions	Yeasts, cereal bran
Molybdenum Selenium Chromium	Appear to have some essential function	Most ingredients contain trace amounts

Feed Formulation and Manufacture

Knowing the requirements of the fish that must be met in the diet, it is possible to compound a feed from various ingredients that will satisfy these. We will show an example of feed formulation based on the approximate analysis of some commonly available substances from the list in table 17. A diet for rainbow trout must contain between 35 and 40% protein, 9—11% lipid, 30—35% total carbohydrate, 1—5% fibre, 1—3% of a commercial vitamin mixture (preferably containing a trace mineral supplement), and no more than 11% of minerals as ash content. Some typically available ingredients would be herring meal, meat and bone meal, brewers yeast, extracted soyabean meal and wheat grain. Following the analyses shown in table 17, the proportions of these ingredients within the diet must be adjusted so that the totals of protein, lipid, carbohydrate, fibre and ash fall within the ranges shown above.

Diet formulation requires a great deal of patience, for the percentage of each ingredient must be altered in turn to try and balance the analysis of the complete diet, and, as a general rule, some sort of fish meal should be included at not less than 20% in all diets.

According to table 17, 20% of herring meal would contribute (% age $\frac{component}{100}$ x desired % age) = 0.767 x 20 or 15.34% for protein, and so on (see table 16). This calculation is performed for all the chosen ingredients, until the sum of each dietary constituent falls within the desired range. The term NFE means 'Nitrogen-free Extractives', which is what is left (largely carbohydrate) after everything else has been analysed. For practical purposes it is considered to be purely carbohydrate.

Table 16 Formulation of a Trout Diet

Protein	Lipid	Fibre	Ash	NFE	Level of ingredient in diet (%)	
15.34	1.64	0.22	2.14	0.68	Herring Meal 20	(21.74)
8.64	0.22	0.58	1.24	7.34	Brewers Yeast 18	(19.35)
6.46	1.21	0.28	3.72	0.34	Meat+Bone Meal 12	(12.77)
5.15	0.10	0.67	0.45	3.43	Extracted Soyabean 10	(11.24)
4.29	0.57	1.02	0.54	23.58	Wheat Grain 30	(33.71)
—	5.00	—	—	—	Cod Oil 5	(5.00)
—	2.00	—	—	—	Corn Oil 2	(2.00)
—		—	1.00	—	Calcium phosphate 1	(1.04)
—	—	—	—	—	Vitamin premix 2	(2.00)
39.88	10.74	2.77	9.09	35.37	100	(107.85)

Nutrient content based on approximate analysis (% of dry ingredients)

The total analysis of the diet falls within the ranges set for each ingredient — in fact, protein need not have been so high, but it would have been difficult to lower it without increasing the carbohydrate content. This diet is only meant as an example of feed formulation and is not necessarily a particularly good diet.

In table 17, Dry Matter Content (%) allows the amount of water

Table 17 Some useful Ingredients and their Composition

Ingredient	Approximate Analysis (% dry weight)							
	Dry Matter (%)	Protein (%)	Lipid (%)	Fibre (%)	NFE (%)	Ash (%)	Calcium (%)	Phosphorous (%)
Alfalfa (plant)	93	16.3	2.5	28.4	44	9.0	1.32	0.24
Blood meal	91	87.8	1.8	1.1	3.1	6.2	0.31	0.24
Meat & bone meal	94	53.8	10.1	2.3	2.8	31.0	11.24	5.39
Barley (grain)	89	13.0	2.1	5.6	76.6	2.7	0.09	0.47
Molasses	77	8.7	0.3	—	80.4	10.6	0.21	0.04
Dicalcium phosphate	96	—	—	—	—	—	23.1	18.6
Whey (dried)	94	14.7	0.9	—	74.1	10.3	0.93	0.84
Skimmed milk (dried)	94	35.6	1.0	0.2	55.1	8.1	1.34	1.10
Citrus pulp	90	7.3	5.1	14.4	66.5	6.7	2.18	0.13
Corn Grits byproduct	90.6	11.8	7.2	5.5	72.7	2.8	0.06	0.58
Corn Gluten meal	91	50.6	—	—	—	2.9	—	—
Corn distillers dried solubles	95.5	29.8	9.4	4.2	48.4	8.6	0.31	1.68
Cottonseed meal	92.5	54.0	1.3	9.2	28.8	6.7	0.17	1.09
Condensed fish solubles	51	61.6	12.7	2.0	4.1	19.6	1.2	1.37
Anchovy meal	93	70.9	5.8	1.1	—	15.3	4.84	3.06
Herring meal	92	76.7	8.2	1.1	3.4	10.7	3.2	2.39
Menhaden salmon meal	92	66.6	8.4	1.1	2.6	21.3	5.97	3.05
White fishmeal	92	68.7	4.8	1.1	1.8	23.6	8.55	3.92
Linseed meal (extctd)	91	38.6	1.9	9.9	43.2	6.4	0.44	0.91
Brewers dried grains	92	28.2	6.7	16.3	45	3.9	0.29	0.54
Oats hulls	93	6.0	2.2	29.0	56.3	6.5	0.17	0.20
Oats (groats)	91	18.4	6.4	3.3	69.5	2.4	0.08	0.47
Peanut meal	92	49.8	8.2	12.0	27.7	—	0.18	0.62
Potato meal	90.3	6.5	0.6	1.6	78.1	13.2	0.08	0.22
Feather meal	94	93.0	2.6	0.6	—	—	0.21	0.89
Rice bran	89	8.2	2.1	10.1	74.6	5.0	0.04	0.29
Rice polish	90	13.1	14.7	3.3	60	8.9	0.04	1.58
Seaweed meal (Fucales)	89.4	10.7	—	8.6	—	—	2.05	0.20
Shrimp meal	90	52.7	3.2	12.2	1.7	—	8.17	1.77
Sorghum (Milo) grain	89	12.4	3.1	2.2	80.4	1.9	0.45	0.33
Soyabean (roasted)	93.6	42.9	19.6	—	—	5.0	—	—
Soyabean (extracted)	89	51.5	1.0	6.7	34.3	6.5	0.36	0.75
Wheat (bran)	89	18	4.6	11.2	59.3	6.9	0.16	1.31
Wheat flour byproduct	89	20.2	4.0	2.2	70.8	2.8	0.09	0.58
Wheat middlings	89	18.9	—	—	—	—	—	—
Wheat grain	89	14.3	1.9	3.4	78.6	1.8	0.06	0.40
Brewers yeast	93	48.0	1.2	3.2	40.8	6.0	0.14	1.54
Torula yeast	93	51.9	2.7	2.2	34.8	8.4	0.61	2.02

in each of the listed ingredients to be taken into account. A 93% dry matter content means that the ingredient contains about 7% water, and the approximate analyses which are based on the average composition of the ingredients are expressed as a percentage of the dry matter content. The column of figures in brackets at the far right of table 16 above are the ingredients corrected for their water content. For example, when making up the diet, to include the correct concentration of fish-meal in the diet which would supply the nutrient content listed in the table, slightly more than 20% is needed to account for the water it contains. If one divides the dry weight percentage calculated in the formulation (i.e. herring meal 20%) by the dry matter content (92%) and then multiplies by 100, this gives the figure 21.74, which is the amount of wet herring meal to use to arrive at a dry weight content in 100g of diet of 15.34g of protein, 1.64g of lipid etc. The levels of calcium and phosphorous are not listed in our dietary formulation, because these are already included in the ash content given in the approximate analysis in table 17.

Preparing the Diets

Having decided upon a formulation, the next problem is to decide in what form it should be fed to the fish. It has to be easily assimilable and should not break down in the water for a considerable period, a quality which is especially desirable for carp in ponds, as well as being convenient to store and handle. As we have already mentioned, commercial feeds are supplied in a variety of particle sizes suited to different fish lengths and come in a 'dry' form containing less than 10% moisture, which is quite acceptable for all the species dealt with in this book.

The bulk of the diet will be needed in the form of pellets, which are manufactured commercially by mixing together all the finely-ground ingredients with a little water and forcing the resultant mash through a die under great pressure. The spaghetti-like strands which are formed are cut into pellets as they emerge from the die. The pressure and consequent temperatures involved cause a change in certain ingredients which binds the dietary ingredients together and renders the pellets water stable. Pellets formed in this way are dense and sink quickly when distributed in a pond or tank, so steam is sometimes used during the extrusion process to 'expand' the pellets with trapped air bubbles, which produces hard, water-stable pellets able to float for a considerable period. The high temperatures involved, especially in the latter process, can cause a dramatic reduction in the vitamin content and the commercial pellets are cooled as quickly as possible to prevent this occurring. Many vitamins are quickly degraded by heat, light or moisture, or contact with the air, which accounts for the relatively short shelf life of commercial diets.

Although home-made pellets cannot be as sophisticated as the

126

commercial variety, it is fairly easy to make pellets with an ordinary home mincer. The chosen ingredients should be finely ground (preferably passed through a 1mm aperture sieve) and mixed thoroughly while they are dry. If any oils are to be added, they should be included at this time and mixed in. The next step is to add water a little at a time until the mixture takes on the texture of a stiff dough. An electric mixer is invaluable at this stage. Too little or too much water makes extrusion of a smooth 'worm' impossible, and the quantity of water required has to be judged by experience. If the diet will not form a dough, then more binding agents are needed. Many substances can be used to fulfill this purpose including yeasts, whey, soyabean meal and wheat flour. There are also several synthetic binders available from chemical manufacturers which are expensive but have the advantage that binding capacity is assured if they are included at the correct levels.

After extrusion of the dough through the mincer, the wet strings of diet should be laid out on sheets of aluminium foil or stainless steel gauze to dry, and separated a little at the same time. They should be air dried, preferably in a stream of cold air (from a household fan) until they contain about 10% moisture. The quantity of the water can easily

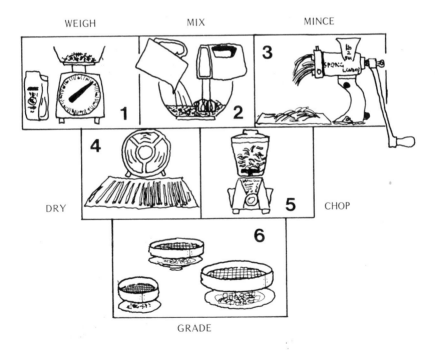

Fig. 35

be determined by placing a weighed sample of the diet in a warm oven overnight, and reweighing in the morning. The diets should be dried as quickly as possible (within twenty-four hours) to prevent the growth of mildew.

Once they are dry, the diets can be broken up in a liquidiser or coffee mill (taking care not to reduce them back to a powder), and then graded into the correct sizes by passing them through suitably sized sieves. The preferred sizes for pellets have been described previously in the section on commercial fish food and these sizes are suitable for all the four species. Any dust or undersized pellets can be reground and repelletised, or added to the next batch. Unfortunately, most home mincers have dies for only two sizes of pellet, but these are normally large enough to suit a wide range of fish sizes. Feeding small pellets

Table 18 Typical Diet Formulations suitable for Catfish, Trout & Carp

| Ingredient | % in Diet | | | | | |
| | Suitable for trout | | Suitable for carp | | Suitable for catfish | |
	Diet 1	Diet 2	Diet 1	Diet 2	Diet 1	Diet 2
Cottonseed Meal		5				20
Maize			25			
Barley			14.5			
Rye Flour			5			
Molasses			5			2
Groundnut Meal	10		5			
Soyabean Meal			5	15	20	
Whey Powder	10		3			
Yeast	4	10	5			8
Fishmeal	31	24	10	10	12	20
Meatmeal	10		10	10		
Bloodmeal			4		10	
Wheat Middlings	20	7		10		20
Rice Bran				25	35	
Rice Polish				20	10	
Distillers Solubles		21		4	8	15
Limestone Flour			1			
Bone Meal		5	1			
Linseed Meal			5			
Lucerne Meal				5		
Liver Meal	5					
Cod Liver Oil	2	3				2
Dried Skim Milk		3.5				10
Alfalfa Meal				4		2
Vitamin Premix	1	1.5	1.5	1	1	1
Cellulose Flour		20				

to large fish, however, can cause a reduction in food conversion, so some care should be taken.

Try to avoid making over-hard pellets, as soft-mouthed fish like carp and tilapia may reject them. On the other hand, very soft pellets disintegrate quickly in water, so a happy medium has to be sought. Both texture and palatability are difficult to predict during diet formulation and pellet acceptibility by the fish is dependent on these factors, so a large amount of trial and error is involved in this aspect of diet manufacture. Diets containing a reasonable proportion of fish meal are usually well accepted, but we have found that diets containing much soyabean meal are poorly accepted, at least by rainbow trout.

Since the same criteria of food storage and shelf life apply to both home-made diets and commercial varieties, no feed should be stored for longer than three months and for that period in cool, dry surroundings. The greatest advantage with home-made diets is of course the ability to make what is needed as and when it is required, thus circumventing storage arrangements.

NUTRITIONAL PROBLEMS

If commercial food is used in accordance with the manufacturer's instructions, then nutritional disorders of the fish should not occur. However, the home formulator could conceivably run into difficulties, so it would be useful to consider here some that might arise.

Problems of Protein Nutrition

A deficiency or imbalance in the protein portion of the diet will be associated with poor growth. This can occur even if the gross protein content of the diet appears to be optimal, because some protein sources can be indigestible or their constituent amino acids unavailable for absorption by the fish. On the other hand, even with a good quality protein source, poor growth may result if dietary energy is too low. Carnivorous animals, and fish are no exception, actually prefer protein as an energy source and dietary energy in the form of carbohydrate or lipid forces the animal to use protein for growth rather than energy only when the protein content of the feed is just sufficient for normal growth. Too low a dietary energy level would thus have a more pronounced growth retarding effect in a carnivorous trout than an omnivorous carp, for example.

Problems of Lipid Nutrition

Apart from their protein sparing action discussed above, lipids supply the essential fatty acids and a deficiency of these can lead to the appearance of certain symptoms as well as reduced growth. Fatty acid deficiency diseases include such things as heart failure and rotting of the caudal fin, and ultimately death.

Excess of fat causes metabolic disorders similar to those found in obese animals and humans, affecting the heart and liver and involving fat deposition in various tissues. Fatty fish are generally unpalatable, although slightly fattier fish than those normally sold fresh to consumers are reckoned to be better for smoking.

Problems of Carbohydrate Nutrition

Trout and catfish are particularly susceptible to carbohydrate excesses, while carp and probably tilapia are much more tolerant in this respect. In trout, excess digestible carbohydrate leads to increased blood sugar levels and increased storage of sugar as liver glycogen, which may eventually cause death through liver malfunction.

Problems of Vitamin Nutrition

As is the case in human and animal nutrition, a deficiency of any of the vitamins in fish diets leads to the appearance of characteristic deficiency disease symptoms. These are the nutritional disorders most likely to be encountered by the farmer, with both commercial and home-made diets, because of the ease with which the vitamins are destroyed. We have therefore prepared a table of the vitamins and their associated deficiency symptoms in an attempt to simplify the account of these.

If any of the symptoms listed in the table are suspected in the fish, then a more detailed text should be consulted to identify positively the deficiency disease involved.

Problems with minerals

Mineral deficiency symptoms are only likely to occur in cases of severe dietary deficiency, because of the ability of fish to absorb minerals directly from the water. Only the major elements calcium and phosphorous are likely to be in short supply, and their absence causes retarded growth.

Of the trace minerals, deficiency syndromes have been demonstrated for iodine and cobalt in fish, and they play the same role in fish nutrition as they do in animal nutrition. Iodine lack leads to goitre, a massive enlargement of the thyroid gland around the gills. Cobalt is involved in vitamin B12 metabolism, and its deficiency symptoms are the same as those for vitamin B12.

Table 19 Vitamin Deficiency and its Symptoms

	Deficiency Symptom								
Vitamin	Skin lesions, darkening	Poor growth	Poor appetite	Eye disease	Nervous disorders	Oedema (pot-belly)	Blood problems	Clubbed gills	Lethargy
Thiamin		+*	+		+	+			
Riboflavin	+	+	+	+			+		
Pyridoxine	+		+		+				
Pantothenate	+	+	+			+		+	+
Inositol	+	+							
Biotin	+	+	+		+				
Folic Acid	+	+							+
Choline		+					+		
Nicotinic Acid		+	+		+	+	+		
Vitamin B12			+				+		
Vitamin C	+			+				+	
Vitamin A		+	+	+		+			
Vitamin K				+			+		
Vitamin E		+				+	+		

* + refers to the presence of a feature.

9 breeding and rearing

The four species require different levels of expertise for their breeding and rearing. Because of their small size and delicacy, all fish larvae are difficult and demanding to look after, and this is not a task that a novice should attempt straightaway. It is better to gain some experience with larger fish before trying to produce and rear one's own to an edible size.

Of the four species, only tilapia will reproduce naturally under intensive farming conditions, a fact which reduces their suitability for fish farming as we have already mentioned. Rainbow trout will mature in captivity, but usually need to have the eggs artificially removed from them and fertilised with milt from a male. Similarly, carp and catfish will mature in captivity if the water is warm enough for long enough, but will never release the eggs in a confined space without a hormone injection that brings about the final ripening of the eggs. Apart from tilapia, sexual maturity is usually reached at a much greater weight for the other three species than our recommended edible sizes, which means brood fish of a fairly large size must be kept in a separate facility if it is intended to produce one's own fry. Special hatching and rearing equipment would also be needed. Below, we have explained in some detail the techniques and equipment required for breeding rainbow trout and tilapia, but have not covered carp and channel catfish because they are much more difficult to breed on a small scale.

THE REPRODUCTION OF RAINBOW TROUT

The spawning season for rainbow trout lasts from about October to the following February or March, and most fish in the wild spawn during December and early January. The availability of fry is therefore seasonal. Although male trout may mature and produce viable sperm during their first year, males and females usually mature towards the end of their second year when they weigh about 300g. Brood stock (especially females) 0.75kg and above are preferred for breeding purposes because their eggs are larger and produce larger, healthier fry. The quality of the hatchlings is very important, large healthy fry being less subject to disease and feeding problems.

Sexually mature males and females, with a little experience, can easily be distinguished. The belly of a ripe female is distended and the vent (the external opening of the oviduct adjacent to the anus) becomes swollen and reddish in colour. Mature young males freely give whitish coloured milt with gentle pressure upon the abdomen, and older males have a pronounced chipe, or extension of the lower jawbone which turns up at the end.

Artificial Fertilisation

The ripe eggs of a female trout lie free in the abdominal cavity and may be expressed from there with a gentle stroking action on the abdomen, termed 'stripping'. After the initial expulsion of the mucous plug which blocks the oviduct, the eggs flow freely, often without assistance, and can be collected in a suitable receptacle such as a plastic basin.

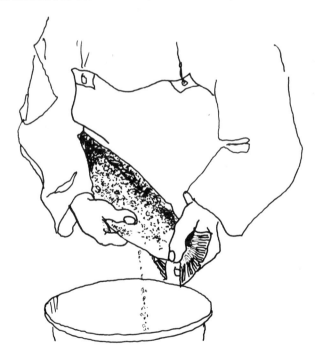

Fig. 36 **Stripping Eggs**

Milt from a male is then stripped in the same way onto the eggs and the two are mixed. Traditionally this was done with a feather, but it is sufficient to gently swirl the bowl. Water is now added a little at a time while the eggs and milt are gently swirled around, until they are covered with 1cm or so of water. They are allowed to stand for about three to five minutes and then washed with two or three changes of water in the bowl. The eggs are heavier than the water, and the cloudy milt and water mixture can be decanted (carefully) without disturbing the eggs. After the washings are completed, the eggs are transferred to a hatching tray supplied with fresh running water where they remain until they hatch.

Incubation and Hatching

The best type of incubation tray allows an even water flow to well up underneath the eggs and overflow past a shallow wier. The current should be just enough to move the eggs slightly in passing, as this ensures that each egg has an adequate supply of well-oxygenated water.

An hour or two after fertilising the eggs and placing them in the hatching tray, they should be examined for any unfertilised or poor quality eggs, which will have turned white. All white or opaque eggs should be removed immediately they are seen, for they are dead and will become infected with fungus. This can spread rapidly from the dead eggs to adjacent living ones and kill them. It is a good preventative measure to bathe the eggs occasionally in a 2ppm solution of malachite green (see the chapter on diseases) introduced with the water flow and gradually allowed to flush out.

The time required for incubation of the eggs until they hatch is dependent on the water temperature, and is often referred to in terms of degree days. For rainbow trout, the period until the absorption of the yolk sac when the larvae become free swimming occupies about 300 degree days, so that at a water temperature of 8°C, (300/8) or approximately 38 days or 6 weeks are required. A week after fertilisation, the eggs become very sensitive to movement and can be easily damaged until the eyes of the larvae start to appear as two black spots about 1mm apart. 'Eyed eggs' require about half the total incubation period to develop, and in this state they are safe to handle and transport. This is the state in which they are generally sold by commercial hatcheries.

Hatching normally extends over a week, and the newly hatched larvae remain passive on the bottom of the incubation tray until their large yolk sac is absorbed, which takes about three weeks at a water temperature of 8°C. The fry then swim up to the water surface and are ready to begin taking food.

Although traditionally fry were fed on minced liver until they were large enough to take other food, commercial fry foods which assure very good survival and growth are now readily available and we would advise the small scale farmer to use these. Fry with absorbed yolk sacs measure about 20mm long, and require feed particles about 0.2 to 0.3mm in diameter. When they reach 30mm, the particle size should be increased to 0.5mm, and to 1mm diameter when they are 40mm long. Artificial food should be distributed at very regular intervals, preferably in small amounts continuously until the fry are 30—35mm long, which requires the use of an automatic feeder of some sort. One can be made very simply from an old clock, as shown in fig. 34. Because the amount of food delivered by an automatic feeder is considerably more than the needs of the fry, and has to be because of their inefficiency in 'catching' their food, screens are very likely to become clogged and should be checked frequently. The larger the area of the screens, the less of a problem this will be, and facilities for holding the fry are best made from two tanks, one inside the other, the inner tank having its bottom completely made of gauze. Water levels can be maintained by a U-shaped pipe draining the outer tank from its centre and discharging into a gutter at the height of the desired water level. Gauze aperture can be increased to 1.5—2mm when the fry have grown to a length of 35–40mm.

The number of eggs yielded by a female trout depends to a large extent on the weight of the fish, but a 1kg fish on average will give about 1,500 eggs. It is easiest to count the eggs when they have eyed, by placing them on a board with a known number of circular depressions. When all the depressions are filled with eggs, the board is emptied and refilled with eggs, and the total number of eggs recorded as a multiple of the number of times the board is filled. It is virtually impossible to count the hatchlings — it is like trying to count ants from a disturbed ants nest. The spawn from three medium sized female trout would be more than sufficient to meet the yearly needs of the small trout farm, with an expected loss of about 30% through the incubation and early rearing period.

THE REPRODUCTION OF CARP AND CATFISH

The natural reproduction of carp and channel catfish in temperate climates is carried out in specially designed spawning ponds, and can occur for a short period each year when water temperatures and other environmental and physiological factors regulating spawning are suitable. Both catfish and carp can be spawned at any time of the year, sometimes several times a year, if they are kept in warm water facilities and given special hormone treatment to induce spawning. The equipment required for this latter process is expensive to set up and maintain, and requires considerable knowledge and expertise for its use, but on the other hand the facilities required for natural spawning require space, which may be at a premium in a back garden.

Spawning ponds of the Dubisch type for carp are small (1 are) square enclosures with a peripheral ditch. They are only 20—30cm deep except in the peripheral ditch, which should be about 80cm deep, and are grassed over for most of the year, preferably with meadow grass (*Lolium perenne*). Dubisch ponds are put under water in the spring when the water temperature reaches a minimum of 18°C and stays there, and stocked with one or two female carp and 3—4 males. Females are recognised by their swollen bellies and males by their production of milt upon gentle pressing of the abdomen. The males usually give milt as soon as the water is warm enough, although the females might be more difficult to recognise. All spawners should be between 3 and 7 years old to assure good quality eggs.

The eggs are laid on the grass or spawning nests made of fibrous material placed in the centre section of the pond, and the ponds are drained when the hatchlings are 2—4 days old. Brood stock are removed immediately after spawning to prevent them damaging the eggs, which hatch after about 4—5 days when the water temperature is 18°C. The fry are tiny (6—8mm long) and the yolk sac is absorbed within two days of hatching, so it is essential to transfer the fry to nursery ponds rich in natural food within four days of hatching. The fry are collected in fine mesh nets from the peripheral ditch after draining the spawning pond; the ditch should be free of all debris and vegetation to facilitate this process.

One female carp produces about 100,000 eggs per kg of body weight, of which 15—30% will probably survive the transferal to the nursey pond. This is a shallow pond about one are in size and 750cm deep which has been well manured or fertilised a week to ten days before stocking with fry. This promotes the production of infusoria and small crustacean zooplankton which form the first food of the fry. Nursery ponds should be thoroughly sterilised before preparing them for stocking, to produce as disease-free an environment for the sensitive fry as possible. Carp larvae during their first three to four weeks will only take natural food, but can be weaned onto artificial food such as trout fry crumbles when they reach 17—18mm length and weigh about 150mg.

Spawning ponds for channel catfish are similar in area to the carp spawning ponds, but slightly deeper, around 60cm. One pair of fish should be stocked per pond when the water temperature reaches 20°C, but some care should be taken to choose fish of comparable size and ripeness, because the male will attack the female (sometimes vice-versa) if they are of greatly different sizes. A spawning receptacle should be placed in the pond, for example a milk churn laid on its side. The eggs will be laid in this and the. male then guards the 'nest' until the larvae are hatched and their yolk sacs absorbed. The male is then removed and the fry, still inside the milk churn, are transferred to a nursery pond.

Female catfish lay their adhesive eggs in a spongy ball containing between 3,000 and 10,000 eggs, and are afterwards driven off by the male who cares for the eggs alone. If both parents are removed after spawning, the egg mass can be transferred to an incubation trough, where the water is agitated to promote oxygenation by a paddle wheel placed to one side of the egg mass. The eggs hatch after 8—10 days, and absorption of the yolk sac is complete after a further week. Four to five days after absorption of the yolk sac, the fry begin feeding and may be fed immediately on artificial diets similar to those employed for rainbow trout.

Induced Spawning

Carp and catfish kept in warm water will mature to the point where the males produce milt and the females assume a swollen belly. However, the females cannot release their eggs because they lack the environmental stimuli which bring about complete ripeness, a hormonal balance which results in the eggs absorbing water and finally ovulation. The eggs of cyprinids and catfish do not lie free in the abdominal cavity, and considerable effort is required by the fish, especially carp, to expel the eggs.

Complete ripeness can be brought about by the administration of fish pituitary sex hormones in both species, although catfish also respond well to mammalian chorionic gonadotrophins. Carp are peculiar in that they usually only respond to pituitary extracts from their own species. The injection of a suspension of dried pituitary extract in 1—2mls of saline or distilled water is most frequently made in the dorsal muscles of the fish, and female carp are given an initial priming dose of a very low concentration some 12—18 hours before the main dose. It is customary to anaesthetise the fish while giving them injections, to facilitate handling.

The priming dose can contain as little as 0.8mg/kg of body weight of the pituitary material, while the main dose is of the order of 3mg/kg of body weight. At the same time as this second injection to the female, the male carp are given a single injection of 0.8mg of pituitary extract, to ensure that good quality, creamy milt is available for fertilisation of the eggs. The female normally gives 'freely flowing' eggs about 6—12 hours after this second injection and these may be fertilised and prepared for incubation. Catfish females can be induced to spawn by a single dose of 1000 IU of human chorionic gonadotrophin, males do not normally need injecting.

The eggs of catfish are fertilised in the same way as those of rainbow trout, allowed to stick together to form the normal spongy mass and incubated in the fashion described above. Carp eggs are more difficult to handle, because of their extreme stickiness. In nature, the female carp releases her eggs a few at a time, and vigorously disperses them over the leaves of submerged plants. This reduces the risk of water deoxygenation around dense clumps of eggs, as well as that of

137

predation and disease transmission. Until a method was discovered comparatively recently for inactivating the sticky layer on the eggs, it was almost impossible to incubate them successfully without huge losses to fungal infections.

Fig. 37 **Preparation of Carp Eggs for Incubation**

At the present time, carp eggs and milt are stripped into a plastic container and mixed by swirling or stirring with a feather. A solution containing 0.3% urea and 0.4% sodium chloride in distilled water is then added in twice the volume of the eggs (approximately). This solution both temporarily reduces the stickiness of the eggs and prolongs the fertilising capacity of the sperms in the milt. More of this solution is added a little at a time as the eggs absorb it, over a period of 1—1.5 hours. The egg container and the treating solution are maintained at 24°C during this period by floating them in a water bath at the requisite temperature, while gently swirling the eggs. After this time, the excess fluid (if any) is decanted and the eggs are quickly rinsed with a 0.15% solution of tannic acid. This is decanted after 10 seconds and the eggs rinsed with fresh water. Two more tannic acid rinses may be given, each rinsed off after 10 seconds, and these have the effect of completely removing the sticky layer from the eggs.

The eggs are now incubated in a large, inverted bottle with the bottom cut off, properly called a Zouger jar. A slow flow of water at 20–26°C is introduced at the bottom of the jar which keeps the eggs in motion, and allowed to overflow at the top. The eggs hatch in this container, and the yolk sac larvae are swept out with the outflow into a suitable rearing tray where they absorb their yolk sac and are fed on live food for two to three weeks, after which time they can be weaned onto artificial diets, or transferred to outdoor ponds.

THE REPRODUCTION OF TILAPIA

Both Java and Nile tilapia are mouth brooders, a term which we have already explained. Only simple aquaria are required for the successful reproduction of tilapia of this type, and the whole process is fascinating to observe.

We mentioned in the section on pond culture of tilapia that a total of three brood pairs of each species would be adequate to supply the next season's stocking material, and these can be housed in two aquaria each holding about 250 litres of water. They should be fitted with a perforated base plate covered with about 2cm of fine gravel and crushed shells, supported 2cm off the bottom of the tank. One corner of this submerged filter plate should be drilled to take a 3cm diameter pipe, which extends from under the plate to just above the surface of the water and contains an airstone about a third of the way up connected to a small aquarium air pump. This effectively makes the aquarium a self contained recycling system, the water passing through the gravel and being pumped onto the water surface by the air-lift pump in one corner, and reoxygenated at the same time. Each aquarium should be fitted with an aquarium heater set to maintain the water at 26°C. A few submerged water plants will make the whole thing more attractive and give the tilapia something to nibble and hide behind.

Three males and females should be stocked in each aquarium, when the males will compete with each other and divide the tank into three spawning territories, the proportion of the tank that these occupy being dependent on the aggressiveness of each male. Although the males will fight, they do not usually harm each other, and a happy medium will be struck after a while. Java males in spawning condition are jet black with bright red spots down either side, but the females retain their normal drab colour.

The male will scoop out a nest in the gravel in the bottom of the tank and a ripe female will deposit the eggs in this depression and then immediately take them up into her mouth. The excited male will then release milt into the nest area and the female takes this into her mouth as well, the fertilisation of the eggs actually taking place inside the female's mouth. About 100 eggs are laid at a time, and these are held in the mouth until the yolk sac is absorbed, some 7 or 8 days. After this, the fry will leave the mother's mouth but will return for progressively shorter periods during the following 10 days. The female cannot eat for this period, which is why tilapia males generally grow faster than the females.

The mouth of the female has an extensible pouch, so that the presence of eggs is easily detected. Should she be netted while in this state, she will spit out the eggs. These may be collected and placed in a net suspended in the aquarium if preferred, where they will develop and hatch quite normally. It is a good idea to separate the fry from the parents in any case, to avoid predation (although this is a fairly remote possibility), and they can be counted and placed in a separate aquarium, smaller in volume but identically set up to the spawning aquaria.

Both species are capable of reproducing every six or seven weeks, and this number of fry will soon mount up. They can be fed on trout fry food and vegetable material, and trout pellets fed to the brood stock will maintain them in good spawning condition through the winter months.

The water in all aquaria should be wholly or partially changed every two weeks, or sooner if it shows any sign of deterioration. Try not to disturb the gravel unless it becomes very clogged, for this will upset the purifying bacteria established within it. The airstones should also be changed every four or five weeks, for they quickly block up and overload the airpump, reducing its working life.

10 diseases

The subject of fish diseases is a complex one, covered in detail in numerous specialist books, but some diseases are more common than others and occur, in one form or another, in most countries of the world. The farmer must be familiar with the symptoms of a few of these diseases, for it is virtually certain that he will encounter some of them at one time or another. Some are easy to identify, others much more difficult, but diagnosis becomes easier with experience.

Disease Prevention
The golden rule of both human and veterinarian medicine applies to fish farming: prevention is always better, cheaper and simpler than cure. Some general points about disease prevention have already been made, but it will be useful to repeat them here.

The first step is to ensure a relatively disease-free water supply. It is important, if water is abstracted from a natural water course containing wild fish, that none of these should ever come into contact with the farmed fish, as they will undoubtedly be host to a wide variety of diseases. Screens on pond inlets are the most effective measures that can be taken. The farmed fish themselves should always be obtained from a reputable source — in Britain, some fish farms hold a government certificate declaring them disease-free, and it is a good idea to obtain fish from such a source, if possible.

Good hygiene is also essential, for dirty equipment and dirty habits can transmit diseases to the fish. Good habits are simple to make, bad ones hard to break. Pond disinfection by fallowing and liming prevents disease being carried over from one year to the next, and all farm equipment should be similarly disinfected each time it is used. Tanks, nets, buckets and boots can be cleaned with dilute bleach or a commercial disinfectant. Caustic soda (sodium hydroxide) as a

141

10% solution is a very good disinfectant for fish farming purposes and is considerably cheaper than commercial ones, but care should be taken not to splash any on clothes because it rots them. All disinfectants should be rinsed off with fresh water after use, because they are toxic to fish, and not very pleasant substances to get on one's hands. Equipment not in use should be stored dry, since this not only preserves the equipment, but also kills off most aquatic disease agents.

Although disease transmission between tanks cannot be avoided in a recycling system, it makes good sense at least to have separate nets for ponds; a disease outbreak in one is then not necessarily transferred to the others.

Preferably, every new batch of fish brought into the farm should go through a quarantine period when they are kept separate from the other fish and observed for possible diseases before being released. Although this means purchasing extra tanks, it is worth the investment, and it need not be an elaborate arrangement. A record should be kept of the fish passing through such a quarantine facility, noting things such as the condition of the animals on arrival, their behaviour and anything unusual.

Treatment in Quarantine

1. Place the new fish in a quarantine system as physically remote from any other fish on the farm as possible. Observe them for any unusual behaviour for at least three days or until they are feeding normally.
2. Starve all the fish for 12 hours and then place no more than six in a separate bath aerated with an aquarium air pump, containing 200 parts per million (ppm) of formalin solution. (See section on disease treatment).
3. Leave the fish in this bath for one hour, or until they appear stressed and gasp for air at the water surface. Then transfer them to another separate tank containing fresh water, and leave them to recover for twenty-four hours.
4. If the treated fish appear healthy after this time, place all the remaining fish in a 200ppm formalin bath for one hour, or until they appear stressed, and then transfer them to a clean, disinfected tank containing fresh water.
5. Repeat this treatment to all the fish on the following day.
6. Allow the fish three days to recover with feeding, and then starve them for twelve hours.
7. Again take a sample of six fish and place them in a separate aerated bath containing 2ppm of zinc-free malachite green solution. Treat them in this way for one hour, or until they appear stressed, and then transfer them to fresh water. Let them recover for twenty-four hours as before.

8.   If the sample fish appear well on the next day, treat all the fish in the same way, transferring to a disinfected tank afterwards.
9.   Repeat the malachite green treatment on three consecutive days, ensuring the fish appear well before repeating a treatment.
10. Keep the fish in quarantine for a further week, feeding and observing them each day for any signs of ill-health or abnormal behaviour. Should any symptoms appear, refer to the diagnosis chart (table 20) after eliminating symptoms due to water quality.
11. If all appears well, the fish may now be transferred to their respective ponds or tanks.

FISH DISEASES

A classification of the different diseases can make rather dry reading, and the next section is meant primarily as a reference and an explanation of some of the terms that may be encountered in more specialised books.

Basically, there are four types of organisms responsible for diseases in fish; parasites, bacteria, viruses and fungi. Although parasites are not strictly organisms as such, it makes a convenient classification. Below we have set out a list of the most common diseases and their causative organisms according to the above classification. Since the surest diagnosis of a disease is identification of the organism responsible, we have illustrated each disease agent, and will later discuss the symptoms to which they give rise.

(1) Parasites

Protozoans (single-celled)
These parasites are usually found externally on the fish, but some occasionally infect internal tissues. A characteristic of these organisms is their ability to form a very resistant resting stage, allowing them to persist after a treatment. Several successive treatments are therefore often required for their eradication.
(i) White-spot or 'Ich' (Ichthyopthirius) Fortunately not many disease organisms are blessed with such an impossible name, but this is the mostly commonly occurring disease of coarse fish and is easily transferred from them to salmonids. As indicated by the common name, the classic symptom of this disease is the appearance of small white spots or pustules on the body surface, covering the eyes in severe cases. A mucous scraping from the body or gills of affected animals reveals the unmistakeable round, slowly-revolving parasite when observed under a hand lens or the low power objective of a microscope. White-spot is about 0.5–1.0mm in diameter and high temperatures around 25°C favour its development.

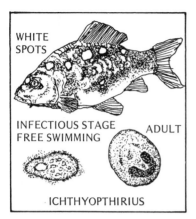

WHITE SPOTS

INFECTIOUS STAGE
FREE SWIMMING

ADULT

ICHTHYOPTHIRIUS

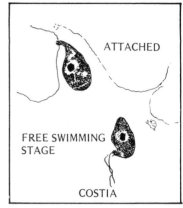

ATTACHED

FREE SWIMMING
STAGE

COSTIA

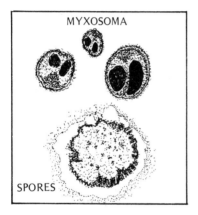

MYXOSOMA

SPORES

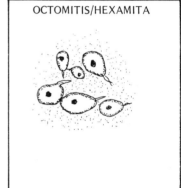

OCTOMITIS/HEXAMITA

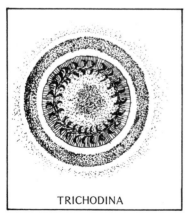

TRICHODINA

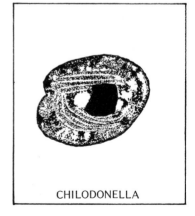

CHILODONELLA

Fig. 38 **Protozoan Parasites**

(ii) **Costiasis (Costia)** This is a severe disease of young fish and fry which may occasionally affect older fish. *Costia* are very small, pear-shaped and possesses two whip-like flagellae with which they propel themselves. They are the same size as the mucous cells in a mucous scraping and thus difficult to observe, except that they move very rapidly. They can only be seen at a magnification of X400 or more, and a good microscope is therefore necessary for their identification. *Costia* are encouraged by acid waters and high temperatures, but can survive temperatures as low as 2°C.

(iii) **Myxosomatiosis or Whirling Disease (Myxosoma)** This is probably the most dangerous disease of young trout caused by a protozoan parasite. It lodges in the cartilage of young fish and spreads through the skeleton causing deformities of the vertebral column. These twists and bends in the spine cause the fish to swim in circles, hence the name of the disease. *Myxosoma* organisms can be found in scrapings taken from the bone at the back of the head, but the spores are tiny and can only be seen at a magnification of X400. The duration of the disease depends upon the rate of growth of the fish, which is linked to temperature and feeding rate, as once the skeleton of the fish has hardened the parasite has a much less drastic effect.

(iv) **Hexamitiasis (Octomitis/Hexamita)** *Hexamita* is a small, active, pear-shaped parasite found in the intestine and gall bladder of fish. It is most often found in salmonids, particularly trout, and can only be seen at X400 magnification or greater, when it is located by its rapid movement. It appears in smears of the gut contents or faeces and usually causes inflammation of the infected organs.

(v) **Trichodiniasis (Trichodina)** These parasites affect the skin and gills and are liable to attack all species of fish. They are large, saucer-shaped and feed off their host by means of rows of rasping teeth. This distinctive parasite can easily be seen under a hand lens or low power of a microscope.

(vi) **Chilodonelliasis (Chilodonella)** Well-known as a killer of fry and fingerlings, this large, slow-moving heart shaped parasite can easily be seen under a hand lens. They are only visible in mucous scrapings from freshly dead or dying fish as they leave the host immediately after its death.

Metazoans (multi-celled)
(i) **Thorny or Spiny-Headed Worms (Acanthocephalus)** These worms parasitise fish intestines and have a hooked proboscis with which they attach themselves to their victim. Before they can infect fish, they must pass a part of their life cycle in an intermediate host, which in this case belongs to the order crustacea. This crustacean host could be a freshwater shrimp or a water louse. Once established, the worms are almost impossible to remove from the fish.

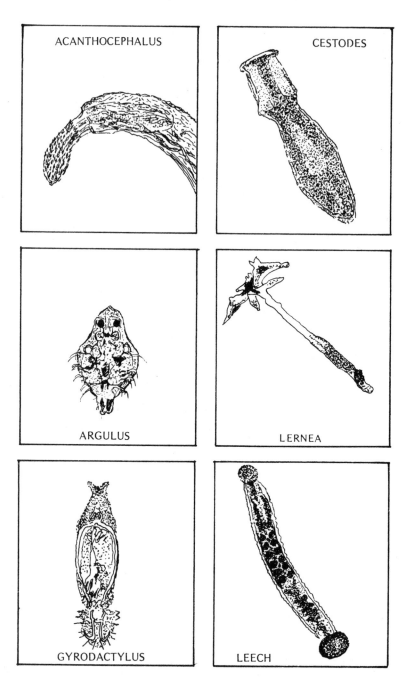

Fig. 39 **Metazoan Parasites**

146

(ii) **Tapeworms (Cestodes)** *Cestodes* are large, segmented flattened worms requiring similar intermediate hosts to *Acanthocephalus*. They vary in shape and length, and have a head bearing suckers or hooks, which is attached to the fish's intestine. They can grow so large that they rupture the gut of their host and invade the abdominal cavity. Their appearance may vary greatly.

(iii) **Crustacea** There are two main crustacean parasites of fish, and these are:

(a) **The Fish Louse (Argulus)** This parasite is found on the body surface, gills and fins of fish. It is about the size of a water flea (3—4mm long) and can be seen with the naked eye as a small speck with two black eyespots.

(b) **The Anchor Worm (Lernea)** The females of this external parasite (the males are not parasitic) have a long worm-like body. They can reach a length of about 20mm, and frequently embed themselves in the fish in the region of the anus.

(iv) **Flukes** There are two important types of fluke:

(a) **Dactylogyrus** Found in the gills, *Dactylogyrus* are about 1mm long with a vicious-looking array of suckers and hooks.

(b) **Gyrodactylus** Similar to *Dactylogyrus* but smaller (0.5—0.8mm) and more often found on the body surface than the gills. They have no dark eyespots, but much more visible hooks than *Dactylogyrus* and are also viviparous, giving birth to live young which can be seen moving around inside older specimens.

(v) **Leeches (Piscicolosis)** Leeches are worm-like with a segmented body, commonly 20—50mm in length, and are easily visible to the unaided eye on the body surface of the fish. Using suckers positioned at both ends of their bodies, they loop around the surface of the fish and may in fact leave their host altogether and swim freely.

(vi) **Larvae of Freshwater Mussels (Glochidia)** Appearing as small white blobs, the larvae of freshwater mussels occur in ponds from May until August each year, predominantly attacking the gills, but they may also be found on the skin of fish.

(2) Bacteria and Viruses

Fortunately only one bacterial disease is likely to affect the fish farm in the normal course of events. If water quality can be ruled out as a source of mortality, and there are no obvious parasitic or fungal infections, then skilled advice should be sought as soon as possible. Many universities, or in Britain, the Government Fish Disease Laboratory, have facilities and staff able to give advice.

Bacterial Diseases

(i) **Aeromonas/Pseudomonas** One bacterium *Aeromonas salmonicida* causes the disease termed furunculosis which usually becomes a problem at higher water temperatures (around 20°C). In young fish, it can cause death with no further symptoms than a period of reduced feeding, but older fish develop boil-like swellings called furuncles, hence the name of the disease. Its presence is most often detected by the putrid smell arising when a freshly dead or dying fish is cut open.

Although other species of bacteria can affect fish, furunculosis is the disease most likely to be encountered, other bacterial diseases being very difficult to diagnose.

Furunculosis

FURUNCLES

Saprolegnia

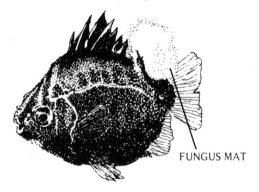

FUNGUS MAT

Fig. 40

Viral Disease

Viruses are the smallest known forms of life and can only be seen and identified by special laboratory techniques. There are no cures for virus infections, and the entire fish stock usually has to be destroyed in an attempt to eradicate the disease and prevent its spread. In Britain, a viral epidemic must be reported to the government who will take measures to contain the outbreak. Four diseases of viral origin are greatly feared among fish farmers, although they do not all occur in the same regions of the world. These are:

(i) **Infections Haematopoietic Necrosis (IHN)** currently confined to North America and Japan, it affects young fish and can cause losses of up to 20% in one day.

(ii) **Infectious Pancreatic Necrosis (IPN)** occurring in North America, Europe and Japan, after initial heavy losses mortalities cease after about four days, but the remaining fish grow poorly.

(iii) **Viral Haemhorragic Septicaemia (VHS)** occurring only in Europe, it affects larger fish and rainbow trout appear to be particularly susceptible.

(iv) **Spring Viraemia of Carp (SVC)** this is presently confined to mainland Europe, where it causes sudden high, sometimes total, losses in young cyprinids when the water temperature rises in the spring. It is also implicated as a cause of the disease referred to as infectious carp dropsy.

(3) Fungi

Although several species of fungi may attach themselves to fish, they are all similar in appearance and *Saprolegnia* species are the commonest. Fungi usually only affect dead tissues, which is why they colonise dead eggs. However, they also attack the site of a wound on a live fish and appear as threads of dirty white or grey. In more serious infections, they look like tufts of dirty cotton wool. Once this stage has been reached, 'sapro' is very difficult to dislodge and distressing to see, and the affected animals may have to be culled.

WHICH DISEASE?

Fish disease diagnosis most often involves the visual recognition of the disease causing organisms, which because of their small size in most cases, requires the use of a microscope. An adequate microscope is liable to be very expensive, and it will be used so infrequently by the fish farmer that it does not seem worth purchasing. One way to get around this problem is to locate some institution that possesses such equipment and arrange for access to it. Local school biology departments almost always have a reasonable microscope and in most cases the teachers responsible will be only too pleased to help.

Diagnostic Procedures
The most important factor here is close daily observation of the fish and their behaviour. The most obvious early warning signs are:
1. A sluggish feeding response.
2. Darkening of the fish — especially noticeable in rainbow trout.
3. Gasping at the surface — associated with respiratory difficulties such as low dissolved oxygen or gill disorders.

4. Abnormal swimming — for example, 'flashing'. In an effort to remove an irritant from the skin, the fish try to rub themselves against the sides or bottom of the tank or pond and in so doing expose a glimpse of their silvery bellies.

Examining the Fish

The examination of dead or unwell fish is a very important part of disease diagnosis, and for such an examination to yield any information, the culturist should know what he is looking at and what he is likely to see.

1. External Examination The main points to note are:

(a) The presence of wounds — perhaps caused by another fish (e.g. fighting amongst male trout causes wounds on the flanks and tail, and raw snouts) or by a predator (fish escaping herons often have parallel scars on either side of the body caused by the bird's beak). Check whether these wounds are infected with fungus, appearing as cotton wool-like strands.

(b) Look for ulceration, white spots, swollen bellies, ragged fins etc., and note the general appearance of the eyes, gills, skin and faeces.

(c) Look for excessive mucous production on the gills and skin. Fish are normally fairly slimy when in good health, but strings of soapy secretions are abnormal.

(d) Search for large Metazoan parasites like leeches, anchor worms and lice.

(e) Lightly scrape a little mucous from the skin of a living or dead fish and place it on a microscope slide with a drop of water, cover with a slip and examine under the microscope, beginning at X100 and working up to X400 magnification. Especially look for anything moving, and try and manouevre to the centre of the stage for closer examination.

(f) Also prepare a slide at the same time of some mucous taken from the gills. They are normally a dark pink colour in living or freshly dead fish, with a light covering of mucous, and go light pink after death or in cases of anaemia. Check whether they have even or ragged margins, and whether there are any white (necrotic) areas or regions of haemorrhaging.

(g) Cut off a small segment of gill tissue in dead fish and look at this under the microscope. Look for 'clubbing' — the pointed normally discrete tips of the gills may become joined to each other or have bulbous ends in certain diseases. This same symptom is also caused by poor water quality, when the gills are subjected to the irritant action of high levels of suspended solids in the water.

Internal Examination Cut open the fish along its ventral side from the anus to a point between the pectoral fins. Now cut from this point up to the lateral line on one side and back along towards the tail and down to the vent, thus removing a flap of muscle and exposing the viscera as shown in the drawing. Try not to cut too deep and disturb any of the internal organs.

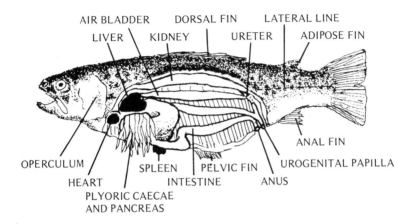

AIR BLADDER   DORSAL FIN   LATERAL LINE
LIVER   KIDNEY   URETER   ADIPOSE FIN

OPERCULUM   SPLEEN   PELVIC FIN   UROGENITAL PAPILLA
HEART   INTESTINE   ANUS
PLYORIC CAECAE
AND PANCREAS

ANAL FIN

Fig. 41

Examine the fish for excessive collection of fluid in the abdomen. Normally, the organs are covered with a thin film of mucous and feel dry to the touch. Also look for haemorrhages, and parasites like tapeworms in the body cavity. If there is fluid in the body cavity, place some on a slide and examine it under the microscope (X400) for bacteria, notably *Pseudomonas/Aeromonas* which may cause the fluid to assume a putrid odour.

Next look at the internal organs; the intestine, liver, kidneys and swimbladder. After gutting a few fish for eating, one becomes familiar with the 'normal' appearance of the organs, and with a little experience it becomes easier to recognise any abnormalities. Prepare slides of the gut contents, kidney and gall bladder by squashing samples under a cover slip — make sure the pressure is applied evenly or it will break.

At each stage of the examination, refer to the disease diagnosis chart below and decide whether any of the symptoms apply to the specimen. Try and identify any organisms observed by comparing them with the descriptions in the preceding section; unfortunately, these can only help to a certain extent, because there is no real substitute for

151

Table 20 Diseases and their symptoms

Disease	Externally Visible Organism	Excessive Mucous Production	Dark Body Colouring	Flashing	Feeding Suppression	Gill Problem Causing Gasping	Wasting	Oedema (Swollen Belly)	Periods of motionlessness and Quivering	Visible External Lesions	Other Distinctive Features	Mortality	Treatment
Ichthyopthirius	–	√√	–	√√	–	√[1]	–	–	–	White spots	–	√	A, B
Costia	√	√√√	–	–	–	–	–	–	–	–	–	√√√	B
Myxosporidia	–	–	√√	–	–	–	–	–	√	Curved backs	Swimming in circles	√	None
Octomitus/Hexamita	–	–	–	–	√	–	√	–	–	–	Gall Bladder— Thick wall and jelly-like contents	√	C
Trichodina	–	√√	–	√	–	√[1]	–	–	–	–	–	√[1]	A, B
Chilodonella	–	√√	–	√	–	√[1]	–	–	–	–	–	√[1]	A, B
Acanthocephalus	–	–	–	–	–	–	√	–	–	–	Visible on dissection	√	D
Cestodes	–	–	–	–	–	–	√	√√	–	–	Visible on dissection	√	D
Argulus	√	–	–	√	–	–	–	–	–	–	–	√[1]	E, F
Lernea	–	–	–	√	–	√	–	–	–	–	–	√[1]	≡
Dactylogyrus	–	–	–	√	–	√	–	–	–	–	–	√	B
Gyrodactylus	–	√	–	√	–	√	–	–	–	–	–	√	B
Leeches	–	–	–	–	–	–	–	–	–	–	–	√[1]	F
Glochidia	–	–	–	–	–	√	–	–	–	–	–	–	–
Aeromonas/Pseudomonas	–	–	√	–	√√	–	–	√	–	White cysts on gills	–	√√	G
IHN	–	–	√√	–	–	–	–	√	–	–	Smell on dissection	√√√	None
IPN	–	–	√√	–	–	–	–	–	–	–	–	√√√	None
VHS	–	–	–	–	–	–	–	√√	–	–	–	√√√	None
SVC	–	–	–	–	–	–	–	√√√	–	–	–	√√	None
Saprolegnia	√	–	–	–	–	–	–	–	–	Fungus balls	–	√[2]	A

SYMPTOMS

Key:
The number of √ denotes the severity of the symptom.

[1] In severe cases only.

[2] As a secondary infection, it may cause mortality.

152

actually seeing an unmistakable specimen of a particular disease causing organism. Once seen, they are never forgotten and will be identified with speed and certainty at another time.

If you are reasonably satisfied that you have identified the disease agent in question, refer to table 20 for the recommended treatment, and then look at the detailed description of the treatment in the following section. Be sure to follow the instructions carefully, because most of the chemicals used are toxic to the fish in concentrations only slightly greater than their therapeutic dosage. They generally rely on poisoning the disease organisms before they quite poison the fish!

DISEASE TREATMENTS

The substances listed below are fairly easy to obtain, with the exception of antibiotics, and are generally accepted as effective treatments when used in the fashion we have described. When bathing or dipping fish in a chemical solution, or adding chemicals to the feed, always be sure to treat a few fish to begin with. This will ensure that the treatment is not more lethal than the disease, and safeguard against errors in administration.

Treatment Key
- A Malachite Green
- B Formalin
- C Enheptin
- D Di-n-butyl tin oxide
- E Potassium permanganate
- F Masoten
- G Antibiotics

A. Malachite Green This chemical is available from most aquarists and chemical suppliers either as a crystalline solid or as a concentrated solution. When buying malachite green, ensure that it is in the zinc-free form, because malachite green containing zinc is very toxic to fish. Do not buy malachite green which is not labelled as zinc-free.

A few grams of this chemical as a solid or a concentrated stock solution will go a very long way, because the recommended dose rates are two parts per million (ppm) for fry and fingerlings, and 1ppm for adult fish. If it is purchased in the solid form, it should be made up into a stock concentrated solution, because the small quantities of the solid required at a time are very difficult to weigh accurately. It is much easier to dilute a solution. A suitable stock solution can be made by dissolving 1g of solid malachite green in 1 litre of water, which will yield a 1000ppm solution. If 1ml of this solution is then added to 1 litre of water, a solution containing 1ppm of malachite green will result, which is a very convenient way of making up treatment baths for the fish. When making up the stock solution, it is a good idea to persuade a chemist to weight out a gram or two accurately if an accurate balance is not available. Always wear rubber gloves when handling this powerful green dye or it will stain the skin for weeks. It may also be harmful in high concentrations, so avoid contact with skin and eyes.

Bath treatments of malachite green should last for one hour or until the fish show signs of stress, whichever is the shorter. However, pond treatment requires a different approach, a combination of a bath and a flush treatment (this simply means gradually flushing out the chemical as soon as it is added to the water). The pond should be drained to half its normal depth by removing the requisite number of boards from the monk, and the amount of malachite green required to give the desired concentration (1 or 2ppm, depending on the size of the fish) in this volume of water is initially mixed up in a dustbin. This is added to the inflow to the pond over a period of 20–30 minutes. After one hour drain the pond to a quarter of its depth while maintaining the inflow at its greatest rate, and replace the monk boards only when the malachite green is obviously greatly diluted. Do not forget to put or leave screens in place in front of the monk when draining the pond, else the fish may leave with the malachite green!

B. Formalin Formalin is the common name for a 40% solution of formaldehyde gas in water, which is readily obtainable from chemists and chemical suppliers. In contrast to malachite green, formalin should always be freshly obtained, because it deteriorates on storage. 'Off' formalin can be recognised by a white or off-white precipitate in the bottom of the bottle, caused by light decomposing the formalin to a substance called paraformaldehyde, which is very poisonous to fish. Formalin should be handled with great care because it gives off a poisonous and irritant vapour which should never be inhaled.

Formalin is used in baths at a concentration of 200ppm in most cases, the 40% solution being considered as 100% for the purpose of concentration calculations. Formalin removes oxygen from the water, so treatment baths should always be well-aerated with an aquarium pump or compressor. Ponds are best aerated at higher water temperatures with a hired compressor. When the concentration of dissolved oxygen in water is reduced, formalin should be used at the lower concentration of 160ppm (above 15°C). When making up a treatment bath, and especially when treating a pond (in the same manner as described for malachite green), one or two drops of a 1000ppm solution of malachite green should be added to the formalin solution. The consequent staining of the water allows the dispersion of the formalin to be observed, and even mixing can thus be effected.

C. Enheptin This is the commercial name for a compound also known as Acinitrasole, and chemically described as 2-amino 5-nitrothiazole. Although more difficult to obtain than the two chemicals described above, Enheptin can be ordered through chemists, or directly from the major drug companies. As a treatment for *Octomitis/Hexamita*, it is added to the feed at a concentration of 0.044g/kg fish/day for five consecutive days.

The Enheptin should be mixed with a little water and this added to the dry pellets or other supplementary food, which are then shaken up in a bucket for five minutes or so to disperse the chemical thoroughly amongst the food.

D. Di-n-butyl Tin Oxide This is used for the eradication of *Acanthocephalus* and cestode parasites of the intestine, and is added to the feed in the same way as Enheptin. It is a slightly more exotic chemical than malachite green or formalin, and will have to be ordered through a chemist or chemical company, but it should not be too difficult to obtain. Di-n-butyl tin oxide should be added to the feed at a rate of 0.252g/kg fish/day, and the treatment again administered for five consecutive days.

E. Potassium permanganate This is readily available from chemists as a purple crystalline solid, and is used for the treatment of *Argulus* infections. A tank containing permanganate solution at a concentration of 1000ppm (1g/litre) is prepared, with a tank containing clean water alongside. A few fish at a time are held in a net and dipped into the permanganate bath for a duration of *10 seconds only*. They are then transferred to the clean water and another batch of fish treated in the same way. Never let the fish out of the net in the permanganate solution, for it is a very deep purple colour and escapees cannot be seen. They will die if they remain in the bath for longer than a minute or two.

F. Masoten This is the name given to a pesticide which is also commercially called Dipterex, Dylon or Neguvon. It is usually obtainable from seed merchants or agricultural suppliers, and should either be employed as a bath for 1–2 hours or applied to ponds in the same manner as malachite green. It can also be sprayed onto the surface of a pond and allowed to dilute out. Whichever way it is used, its therapeutic concentration is 0.25ppm given twice, the second application being seven days after the first.

G. Antibiotics Antibiotics are added to the feed and applied in a similar fashion to Enheptin, but they are only available on veterinary prescription and the farmer would be advised to seek the advice of a local veterinary surgeon if bacterial infections are suspected.

Concentration Calculations

(a) **Malachite Green Baths** One milligram (0.001g) of solid malachite green crystals in 1 litre of water gives a concentration of 1ppm, but this is such a small amount to weigh that it is better to make up a 1000ppm stock solution, containing 1g of the chemical in 1 litre of water.

> 1 ml of 1000ppm stock solution in 1 litre = 1ppm
> ∴ 2 ml of 1000ppm stock solution in 1 litre = 2ppm
> ∴ 80 ml of 1000ppm stock solution in 40 litres = 2ppm

A 40 litre container is usually adequate as a treatment bath.

(b) **Pond Treatment with Malachite Green**

A one are pond when half-full contains:

> 10 x 10 x 0.5 metres = 50 cubic metres
> 1 m^3 = 1000 litres ∴ 50 m^3 = 50,000 litres.

To obtain a 1ppm solution of malachite green in this volume, 50,000mg or 50g of the solid chemical would be required, or 50,000 ml (50 litres) of the 1000ppm stock solution.

(c) **Formalin Baths** To prepare 40 litres of a 200ppm bath:

> 1 ml in 1 litre = 1000ppm
> 0.2 ml in 1 litre = 200ppm
> 8 ml in 40 litres = 200ppm

(d) **Pond Treatment with Formalin** Required concentration 200ppm, with the same pond dimensions as above:

> 0.2 ml in 1 litre = 200ppm
> 0.2 x 50,000 = 10,000 ml = 10 litres of 40% formalin

Ten litres of formalin mixed up in a dustbin full of water and added to the pond inflow would yield a concentration of 200ppm, gradually diluted by the inflow for one hour and flushed out at the end of this period by further lowering of the water level in the pond.

11 the fish farmer and the law

Anyone planning to rear fish in anything other than domestic aquaria, in Britain and the USA, may have to fulfil certain legal obligations and the first thing anyone planning to keep fish for eating should do is check up on the national and local laws that may apply. In Britain particularly, current laws are likely to be changed in the near future to rectify the somewhat ambiguous position that fish farming occupies at the moment.

THE LAW IN BRITAIN

There are four major Acts of Parliament which contain clauses of direct interest to fish farmers, together with a few minor ones that might apply. These are the Town and Country Planning Act (1971), the Salmon and Freshwater Fisheries Act (1975), the Prevention of Pollution Act (Rivers Act 1951) and the Water Resources Act (1963).

The Town and Country Planning Acts

These acts relate to the granting of planning permission for any type of land development. Agriculture, the definition of which under the Act includes the phrase 'the keeping of livestock for food' is specifically exempted from planning permission, which suggests aquaculture should be exempt too. However, the British Government does not recognise aquaculture as a form of agriculture at the present time, and this tends to confuse things a little. The Act is most likely to apply if ponds are being dug, since any excavation requires planning permission from the local planning authority. Damming a water course to supply water for the ponds would also require planning permission, as well as the authorisation of the Regional Water Authority.

The Salmon and Freshwater Fisheries Act

This Act was primarily designed to protect and preserve natural fish stocks, and certain clauses are likely to apply to the fish farmer if he interferes with a natural water course for the benefit of his fish farm. Damming a natural trout or salmon stream may interfere with their up-stream migration during spawning time and, under the Act, owners or occupiers of the land on which the dam is constructed must install and maintain a fish pass for migrating salmonids according to the specifications of the Ministry of Agriculture, Fisheries and Food (MAFF). This same clause also applies to the alteration of any existing dam for any purpose.

In addition, the Act covers the release (accidental or deliberate) of fish or eggs from a fish farm into a natural water course. It is an offence under the Act to release fish or spawn into a water course without prior permission in writing from the Regional Water Authority. The Water Authority must in any case be informed of the intention to keep fish in water under their jurisdiction, and they will probably make an appropriate ruling for an individual case (especially if tilapia are kept in an outdoor pond).

The Rivers (Prevention of Pollution) Act and the Water Resources Acts

Since these both apply to water extraction and disposal, we will consider them together. It is necessary to obtain a license from the Regional Water Authority for:

(1) The construction or alteration of any form of dam or wier or other obstruction across a water course intended to impound water along that water course. Impoundment of water that is not part of a defined inland water or water course (such as surface runoff) may not require a license, but the Water Authority should be approached in any case.

(2) Abstraction of water from an inland water source, including surface and underground water. Usually a charge is made proportional to the amount of water abstracted on a continuous basis. Abstraction of water from the domestic supply also requires a license and may be metered depending on its volume (largely at the discretion of the Water Authority). The Water Authority should be informed of the intention to use the domestic water supply for a small scale recycling system, and asked for their permission. Since no specific clauses or test cases relate to this subject, it is again at the discretion of the Water Authority as to whether a license and tariff are required. Most Water Authority personnel are interested and helpful on this topic.

3) Discharge of fish farm effluent into a natural water course. The waste water from a farm is considered as a 'trade effluent' because of its content of ammonia, waste food etc., which would reduce the quality of water in a natural water course. Irrespective of whether a trade effluent is involved or not, the prior consent of the Water Authority is

required under Land Drainage bye-laws if water is discharged into a main river.

In addition to the Acts mentioned above, there may be local bye-laws that relate to water abstraction, or to use of land for keeping livestock, and the local borough authority should be approached in this connection. The other most important point of law concerns the so-called 'Riparian rights' of a landowner. These confer on the owner of land on the banks of a stream the right to have that stream enter and leave his property in its natural state with regard to flow rate and water quality. This means a Riparian owner has the right to contest use of the water by another, if that person interferes with the stream in any way, and alters its natural qualities. A fish farm drawing and discharging water from and into a stream is bound to have some effect on the water, so Riparian rights can be very important indeed. Although a Riparian owner has the right to the reasonable use of the water while it is flowing past his land, including its use for domestic purposes and for turning mills etc., as long as there is no reasonable interference with the rights of superior (upstream) and inferior (downstream) users, it is questionable whether use for a fish farm is reasonable. Generally, use of Riparian water outside the Riparian land would be considered unreasonable.

Riparian rights also apply to underground water flowing in defined channels, but not to subterranean water diffused through the strata, or to diffuse surface water not occupying definable natural channels.

Tenants or occupiers leasing land from owners should also check that the terms of the tenancy or lease agreement do not preclude the building of a fish farm on the land. Proposals for development should be approved by the owners of the land before any work begins.

There are regulations applying to the use of sea water for marine fish farming, but since this is a subject not covered by this book, they will not be considered here.

THE LAW IN THE USA

Because of the existence of different laws in different states, the legal picture in the USA is rather more complicated than in Britain. No federal laws apply directly to the private farming of fish, but other federal laws related to land and water use, environmental protection and health and safety affect private aquaculture. Most of the laws that specifically permit, control or prohibit fish farming are at the state level, and are linked with state authorities managing fisheries resources and conservation. We cannot possibly cover all the different laws in different states, but we have tried to describe the types of legal requirements commonly affecting the fish culturist in the majority of states.

Because aquaculture is concerned with food production, water supply, the use of navigable waters and effluent discharge, it is regulated by agencies involved with public health, water purity, land use and pollution control, and regulations sometimes occur at all three levels of government, federal, state and local. Federal laws dealing with public health and safety, such as the Federal Food, Drug and Cosmetic Act need to be considered where any fish are offered for sale. Bear in mind, however, that it may be illegal to use certain common chemicals for disease treatment which have not been approved by the Food and Drug Administration.

In some states, laws designed for public fisheries resource management have not been revised to take fish farming into account, and state laws applying to conservation of natural stocks prohibit private culture and ownership of certain fish species. Permits, licences and periodic reports are required by state agencies for their administration of laws specifically related to aquaculture as well as laws related to land and water use. In several states, more than thirty such requirements must be met before an individual can legally commence rearing fish.

Problems of Land Use

Apart from common law rights to land, involving public access to land and restrictions on land use tied to property deeds, zoning ordinances may affect land use for aquaculture. Zoning designations, enforcable by the police, are often made under the guidelines of a local master plan. If aquaculture has not been considered during the drawing up of these plans, some difficulties might be encountered in reconciling fish farming with existing categories of land use. State land management schemes may also affect private aquaculture through zoning if the land area concerned is of particular environmental or historical significance.

Problems of Water Use

Riparian rights, imported almost unchanged from English law, apply in the majority of states, and a Riparian owner can divert water for a 'reasonable' use on the area of Riparian land. The Riparian system makes it difficult to judge what use or volume of water can be considered reasonable, a decision that can only be made by a court faced with a contestation of water use, based on an evaluation of the circumstances confronting all the owners and their conflicting interests.

This inadequacy of the riparian doctrine has prompted several western states with limited water resources to abandon it in favour of an appropriation doctrine, which essentially grants a prior user of water superior rights over a subsequent user so long as the prior user continues to apply the water for a beneficial use. In some states (e.g. North and South Dakota, Oklahoma and Oregon), both riparian and appropriation doctrines co-exist, limiting the exercise of riparian rights.

Should a water supply be taken from navigable waters, and involve the construction of a dam or weir, federal approval through the US Army Corps of Engineers would be required, together with the permission of the state government. Obstruction of riparian waters with a dam or weir should not hinder the free passage of fish up and down the waterway, otherwise action may be initiated under common law to remove such an obstruction.

Under the Federal Water Pollution Control Act, any discharge of a pollutant from a point source into US waters requires a permit issued by the Environmental Protection Agency (EPA) or from a state agency authorised by the EPA to issue such permits. The EPA has not yet proposed guidelines for effluent standards for aquatic animal production, and emission standards are determined for individual permits by the EPA regional administrator. However, in 1976 the EPA redefined aquaculture facilities to exclude certain small operations and such a fish farm may be exempt from National Pollutant Discharge Elimination System permits, although commercial operations without exception require such a permit.

Public health agencies have the power to prohibit water abstraction if the source water is contaminated with sewage, pesticides etc., although few people would want to use such a source in any case!

Advisory Services

As with the situation in Britain, aquacultural advisory services are virtually non-existent (at least, free ones) and the help and advice available to the agriculturist or livestock farmer is limitless in comparison. In theory, the Agricultural Extension Service of the US Department of Agriculture should provide advice for fish farmers, but in practice existing extension offices are often neither prepared or inclined to help. Some help may be available from the extension services provided by the US Fish and Wildlife Service of the Department of the Interior.

It is extremely difficult to obtain lists of the legal permits required or other legal obligations to be fulfilled, within a state. At the state level, a branch of a state natural resources or environmental protection agency may serve the function of a clearing house to inform interested parties of the environmental permits required.

In some states, fishery agencies and university extension services have performed an advisory service explaining environmental, health and consumer laws to inquirers.

If the opportunity to seek advice from someone involved with commercial aquaculture occurs, take it; they will have experienced the permit system and may be able to give a few valuable hints.

Some considerable simplification and unification of aquacultural legal requirements can be hoped for in the future due to the recent (1977) Food and Agriculture Act. This has assigned responsibility for aquacultural matters to the US Department of Agriculture, instead of the several federal departments involved at the present time. Already, recommendations for improvement of the current status of aquaculture have been submitted to this lead agency, and it is to be hoped that they will be implemented in the future.

bibliography

Fish Farming — General Texts

Bardach, J.E., Ryther, J.H., & McLarney, W.O. 1972. *Aquaculture: The Farming and Husbandry of Freshwater and Marine Organisms*. 868p. WileyInterscience, New York.
A comprehensive survey of fish farming throughout the world. Fascinating to read, but not cheap to buy and not too useful from a practical viewpoint.

Bardach, J.E. 1968. Aquaculture. *Science*, 161:1098–1106.
A somewhat dated although still interesting summary of global fish farming and its prospects.

Halver, J.E. (ed.) 1972. *Fish Nutrition*. 713p. Academic Press, New York. Includes information on fish husbandry related to feeding. Good, but very detailed and expensive.

Huet, M. 1970. *Textbook of Fish Culture: Breeding and Cultivation of Fish*. 436p. Fishing News (Books) Ltd., Surrey, England.
Probably the best general text, packed with useful information and photographs, but again expensive. Particularly informative about breeding and early rearing of farmed fishes.

Mendola, D. 1978. Aquaculture: Bringing it Home with the New Alchemists. *Energy Primer*, Merrill, R., & Gage, T. (eds.), Dell Publishing Co. Inc., New York, Prism Press: 183–195
A stimulating look at small scale aquaculture with a useful bibliography.

Roberts, R.J. (ed.) 1978. *Fish Pathology*. 1978p. Bailliere Tindall, London. A most complete treatise on fish diseases and an important reference work, but prohibitively expensive.

Periodicals

Fish Farmer. Agricultural Press Ltd., Surrey, England. (bi-monthly). Coverage of current events in Britain and Europe.

Fish Farming International. Arthur J. Heighway Publications Ltd., London. (quarterly). Coverage of international events of general interest.

Ponds

(1) Construction

Mitchell, T.E. & Usry, M.J. 1967. *Catfish farming – a profit opportunity for Mississippians.* Mississippi Research and Development Centre, Mississippi. 83p

Pruginin, J., & Ben Aria, A. 1959. Instructions for the construction and repair of fish ponds. *Bamidgeh,* 11(1):25–28.

Saha, C., & Gopalakrishnan, V. 1975. Construction of fish ponds. *Journal of the Inland Fisheries Society of India,* 6:122–130.

(2) Fertilisation

Ball, R.C. 1949. Experimental use of fertiliser in the production of fish food organisms and fish. *Michigan State College Agricultural Experiment Station Technical Bulletin* No. 210. 28p.

Fijan, N. 1966. Problems in carp fish-pond fertilisation. *FAO World Symposium on Warm Water Pond Fish Culture,* Rome, 18–25 May, 1966. FR:V/E–4.

Swingle, H.S., & Smith, E.G. 1939. Increasing fish production in ponds. *Transactions of the 4th North American Wildlife Conference.* American Wildlife Institute, Washington, D.C.

Walny, P. 1966. Fertilisation of warm water fish ponds in Europe, *FAO World Symposium on. Warm Water Pond Fish Culture,* Rome, 18–25 May, 1966. FR:II/R–7.

Diseases

Bauer, O.N., Musselius, V.A., & Strekov, Yu.A. 1973. *Diseases of Pond Fishes.* Translated by A. Mereade. Theodor, O. (ed.) Israel Programme for Scientific Translations, Jerusalem.

Herman, R.L. 1970. Prevention and control of fish diseases in hatcheries. *A Symposium on Diseases of Fishes and Shellfish,* Snieszko, S.F. (ed.), American Fisheries Society, Washington, D.C. p3–15.

Hoffman, G.L., & Meyer, F.P. 1974. *Parasites of Freshwater Fishes.* 224p. TFH Publications Inc., New Jersey.

Roberts, R.J., & Shepherd, C.J. 1974. *A Handbook of Trout and Salmon Diseases.* 168p. Fishing News (Books) Ltd., Surrey, England.

Legal Requirements

National Research Council. 1978. *Aquaculture in the United States. Constraints and opportunities.* National Academy of Sciences, Washington, D.C. pp. 74—102.

Rainbow Trout

(1) In Ponds

Leitritz, E. 1972. Trout and salmon culture. State of California Department of Fish and Game, *Fish Bulletin* No. 107. 36p.

Drummond Sedgwick, S. 1976. *Trout Farming Handbook.* 163p. Seeley, Service & Co., London.

(2) In Recycling Systems

Brauhn, J.L., Simon, R.C., & Bridges, W.R. 1976. Rainbow trout growth in circular tanks: consequences of different loading densities. *Technical Papers of the US Fisheries and Wildlife Service,* No. 86. 16p.

Hill, T.K. 1976. An experiment in growing rainbow trout in recirculated water. *FAO Technical Conference on Aquaculture,* Kyoto, Japan, 26 May 1976. FAO—FIR: AQ/Conf/76/E.27.

Meade, T.L. 1974. The technology of closed system culture of salmonids. *Rhode Island University Marine Technical Report,* No. 30. 31p.

Carp

(1) In Ponds

Alikunhi, K.H. 1966. Synopsis of biological data on the common carp. *Cyprinus carpio* (Linnaeus 1758)—Asia and the Far East. *FAO Fisheries Synopses* 31.1.79p.

Nambiar, K.P.P. 1970. Carp culture in Japan—a general study of the existing practices. *Indo-Pacific Fisheries Council, Occasional Paper* 1970/1. 41p.

Sarig, S. 1966. Synopsis of biological data on the common carp, *Cyprinus carpio* (Linnaeus 1758)—Near East and Europe. *FAO Fisheries Synopses* 31.2.42p.

(2) In Recycling Systems

Meske, C. 1968. Breeding carp for reduced number of intermuscular bones, and growth of carp in aquaria. *Bamidgeh,* 20(4):105—119.

Meske, C. 1973. *Aquakultur von Warmwasser — Nutzfishchen.* 163p. Eugen Ulmer, Stuttgart.

It is understood that an English translation of this excellent book on carp culture is in preparation and will shortly be published.

Meske, C. 1976. Fish culture in a recirculating system with water treatment and activated sludge. *FAO Technical Conference on Aquaculture,* Kyoto, Japan, 26 May 1976. FAO–FIR: AQ/Conf/ 76/E.62.

Channel Catfish

(1) In Ponds

Andrews, J., Knight, L., & Murai, T. 1972. Temperature requirements for high density rearing of channel catfish from fingerling to market size. *Progressive Fish Culturist,* 34(4):240–241.

Andrews, J.W., Murai, T., & Gibbon, G. 1973. The influence of dissolved oxygen on growth of channel catfish. *Transactions of the American Fisheries Society,* 102(4):835–838.

Brown, E.E., LaPlants, M.G., & Covey, L.H. 1969. A synopsis of catfish farming. *University of Georgia College of Agriculture Experiment Stations Bulletin* No. 69. 50p.

Lee, J.S. 1971. *Catfish farming.* Mississippi State University Curriculum Co-ordinating Unit for Vocational–Technical Education, State College, Mississippi. 103p.

(2) In Recycling Systems

Andrews, J.W. 1972. Stocking density and water requirements for high density culture of channel catfish in tanks or raceways. *Feedstuffs,* 44(6):40–41.

Lewis, W.M., Yopp, J.H., Schramm, H.L.Jnr., & Brandenburg, A.M. 1978. Use of hydroponics to maintain quality of recycled water in a fish culture system. *Transactions of the American Fisheries Society,* 107(1):92–99.

Parker, N.C., & Simco, W.A. 1973. Evaluation of recirculating systems for the culture of channel catfish. *Proceedings of the 27th Conference of the South-Eastern Association of Game and Fish Commissioners,* Hot Springs, Arkansas, 14–17 October, 1973. Mitchell, A.L. (ed.). p474–487.

Tilapia

(1) In Ponds

Ballarin, J.D. 1979. *Tilapia: A guide to their biology and culture in Africa.* University of Stirling. 174p.

Kirk, R.T. 1972. A review of recent developments in Tilapia culture with special reference to fish farming in the heated effluents of power stations. *Aquaculture*, 1(1):45—60.

Shell, E.W. 1967. Relationship between rate of feeding, rate of growth and rate of conversion in feeding trials with two species of tilapia, *Tilapia mossambica* (Peters) and *Tilapia nilotica* (Linnaeus). *FAO Fisheries Report* 44(3):343—345.

Smitherman, R.D. Shelton, W.L., & Grover, J.H. (eds.) 1978. *Proceedings of the Symposium on the Culture of Exotic Fishes*, Atlanta, Georgia, 4th Jan. 1978. Fish Culture Station, American Fisheries Society, Auburn, Alabama. p 1—108.

(2) In Recycling Systems

McLarney, W.O., & Todd, J. 1974. Walton Two: A complete guide to backyard fish farming. *Journal of the New Alchemists*, p. 77—117.

Recycling Systems

Carmignani, G.M., & Bennett, J.P. 1977. Rapid start-up of a biological filter in a closed aquaculture system. *Aquaculture*, 11:85—88.

Haug, R.T., & McCarty, P.L. 1972. Nitrification with submerged filters. *Journal of the Water Pollution Control Federation*, 44(11): 2086—2102.

Hirayama, K. 1974. Water control by filtration in closed culture systems. *Aquaculture*, 4:369—385.

Kalinowski, P.M. 1975. Recirculation systems for coarse fish rearing. *Proceedings of the 7th British Coarse Fish Conference*, Liverpool, March 1975. p. 63—71.

Liao, P.B., & Mayo, R.D. 1974. Intensified fish culture combining water reconditioning with pollution abatement, *Aquaculture*, 3:61—85.

Muir, J.F. 1976. How filters improve water quality for fish farmers. *Fish Farming International*, 3(3):35—38.

Scott, K.R., & Gillespie, D.C. 1972. A compact recirculation unit for the rearing and maintenance of fish. *Journal of the Fisheries Research Board of Canada*, 29(7):1071—1074.

Speece, R.E. 1969. U-tube oxygenation for economical saturation of fish hatchery water. *Transactions of the American Fisheries Society*, 98:789—795.

Speece, R.E. 1973. Trout metabolism characteristics and the rational design of nitrification facilities for water re-use in hatcheries. *Transactions of the American Fisheries Society*, 102(2):323—334.

Spotte, S.H. 1970. *Fish and Invertebrate Culture: Water Management in Closed Systems*. 145p. John Wiley & Sons, Inc., New York.

Fish Nutrition and Feed Formulation

Boonyaratpalin, M., & Lovell, R.T. 1977. Diet preparation for aquarium fishes. *Aquaculture*, **12**:53–62.

Cowey, C.B., & Sargent, J.R. 1972. Fish Nutrition. *Advances in Marine Biology* **10**:383–492.

Cowey, C.B. & Sargent, J.R. 1977. Lipid nutrition in fish. *Comparative Biochemistry and Physiology*, **57**(b):269–273.

Cowey, C.B., & Sargent, J.R. 1979. Nutrition. *Fish Physiology*, Hoar, W.S., & Randall, D.J. (eds.), **VIII**:p 1 69. Academic Press, New York.

Dabrowski, K.R., 1979. Feeding requirements of fish with particular attention to common carp. A review. *Polish Archives of Hydrobiology*, **26**(1/2):135–158.

Halver, J.E. 1976. Formulating practical diets for fish. *Journal of the Fisheries Research Board of Canada*, **33**:1032–1039.

National Research Council. 1973. *Nutrient Requirements of Trout, Salmon and Catfish.* 57p. National Academy of Sciences, Washington, D.C.

National Research Council. 1977. *Nutrient Requirements of Warmwater Fishes.* 78p. National Academy of Sciences, Washington, D.C.
The above two publications are invaluable when formulating practical diets for fish.

Robinson, P.A. 1970. The what, how and why of pelleting. Report of the 1970 Workshop on Fish Feed Technology and Nutrition, US Department of the Interior Fisheries and Wildlife Service. *Bureau of Sport Fisheries and Wildlife Research Report* No. 102. 20p.

Breeding and Rearing

Horvath, L. 1978. The rearing of warmwater fish larvae. *FAO–EIFAC Symposium on Finfish Nutrition and Feed Technology*, Hamburg, 20–23 June, 1978. EIFAC/78/Symp:R/12.1.

Huisman, E.A. 1973. Hatchery and nursery operations. *EIFAC Workshop on Controlled Reproduction of Cultivated Fishes*, Hamburg, 21–25 May, 1973. pp 102–110.

index

Fishmeal 117–9
Flashing 150
Flow rate 31, 50, 61, 100
Flukes **146**, 147
Food & Agriculture Act 161
Food conversion 2, 36, 52
Formalin 142, 154
Freezing 33, 76
Fry 74, 134–5
Fungi 149
Furunculosis **148**

Galvanised iron 49, 85
Gills 12, 150
Glochidia 147
Gravel 82, 98
Greenhouses 66–7, 72
Growth rate 39–43, 57, 65, 68–9, 72
Gyrodactylus **146**, 147

Hand feeding 47, 71, 115
Hatching 134–40
Header tanks 86, 99
Heating 8, 108–9
Heterotrophic bacteria 80
Hexamita **144**, 145
Holding tanks 33
Horizontal screens **27**
Hygiene 45, 141

Ichthyopthirius 143, **144**
Ictalurus punctatus – see Channel catfish
Incubation 134, 138
Induced spawning 135–9
Insulation 109
Intensive husbandry 2

Java tilapia **10**, 9–11, 71–6, 112–14, 139–40

Kainit 63

Larval rearing 113
Lates niloticus – see Nile perch

Leeches **146**, 147
Legal requirements 14, 157–61
Lernea **146**, 147
Levelling 21
Lice **146**, 147
Lime 35, 62, 75
Lipids 118, 129

Malachite green 142, 153–4
Management of ponds – see Ponds
Masoten 155
Metazoa 145
Milt 133–4
Minerals 122–3, 130
Mirror carp 7, 7–8, 57–67, 108–12, 135–9
Monk **24–6**, 33, 58
Mortality 36–7, 41, 49, 73, 102
Mouth brooding 139
Myxosoma **144**, 145

Natural productivity 34, 61–2
Neguvon – see Masoten
Nile perch 74
Nile tilapia **10**, 9–11, 71–6, 112–14, 139–40
Nitrate 80
Nitrification 80–1
Nitrifying bacteria 79–80
Nitrite 80
Nitrobacter – see Nitrifying bacteria
Nitrogen cycle **80**
Nitrosomas – see Nitrifying bacteria
Nutrition 116–31

Octomitis **144**, 145
Oscar's cichlid 74
Oxygen 4, 12, 16, 80, 87, **90**, 93
– demands 63, 79, 88–91
– transfer 12, 50, 87

Parasites 143
Pellets 52–6, 75, 114, 126